top shelf
productions
presents

PUBLISHED BY TOP SHELF PRODUCTIONS, PO BOX 1282, MARIETTA, GA 30061-1282, USA. PUBLISHERS: BRETT WARNOCK AND CHRIS STAROS.

VISIT OUR ONLINE CATALOG AT WWW.TOPSHELFCOMIX.COM.

FIRST PRINTING, APRIL 2009. PRINTED IN CANADA.

Second thoughts

by niklas asker

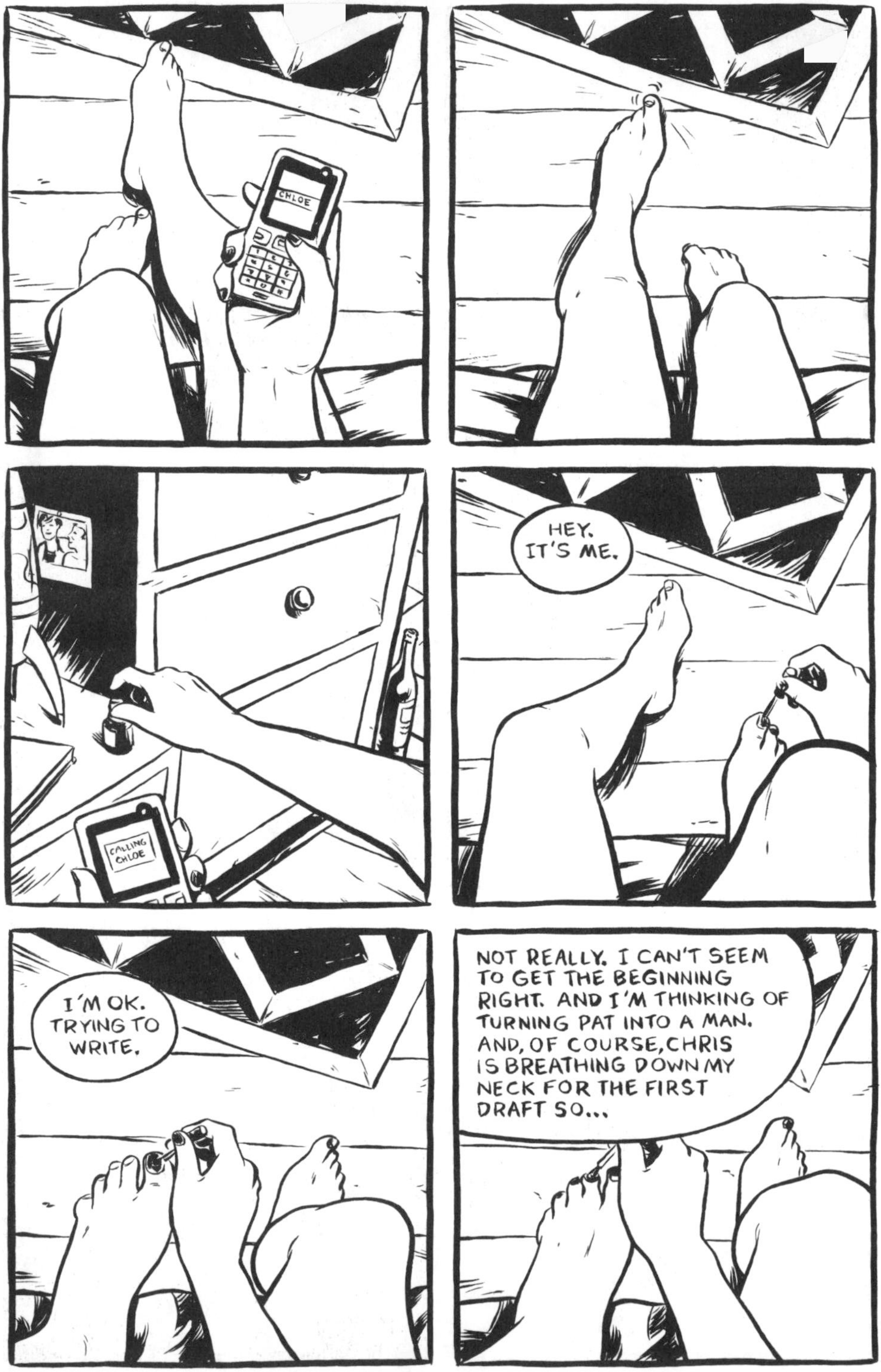
CHLOE
CALLING CHLOE
HEY. IT'S ME.
I'M OK. TRYING TO WRITE.
NOT REALLY. I CAN'T SEEM TO GET THE BEGINNING RIGHT. AND I'M THINKING OF TURNING PAT INTO A MAN. AND, OF COURSE, CHRIS IS BREATHING DOWN MY NECK FOR THE FIRST DRAFT SO...

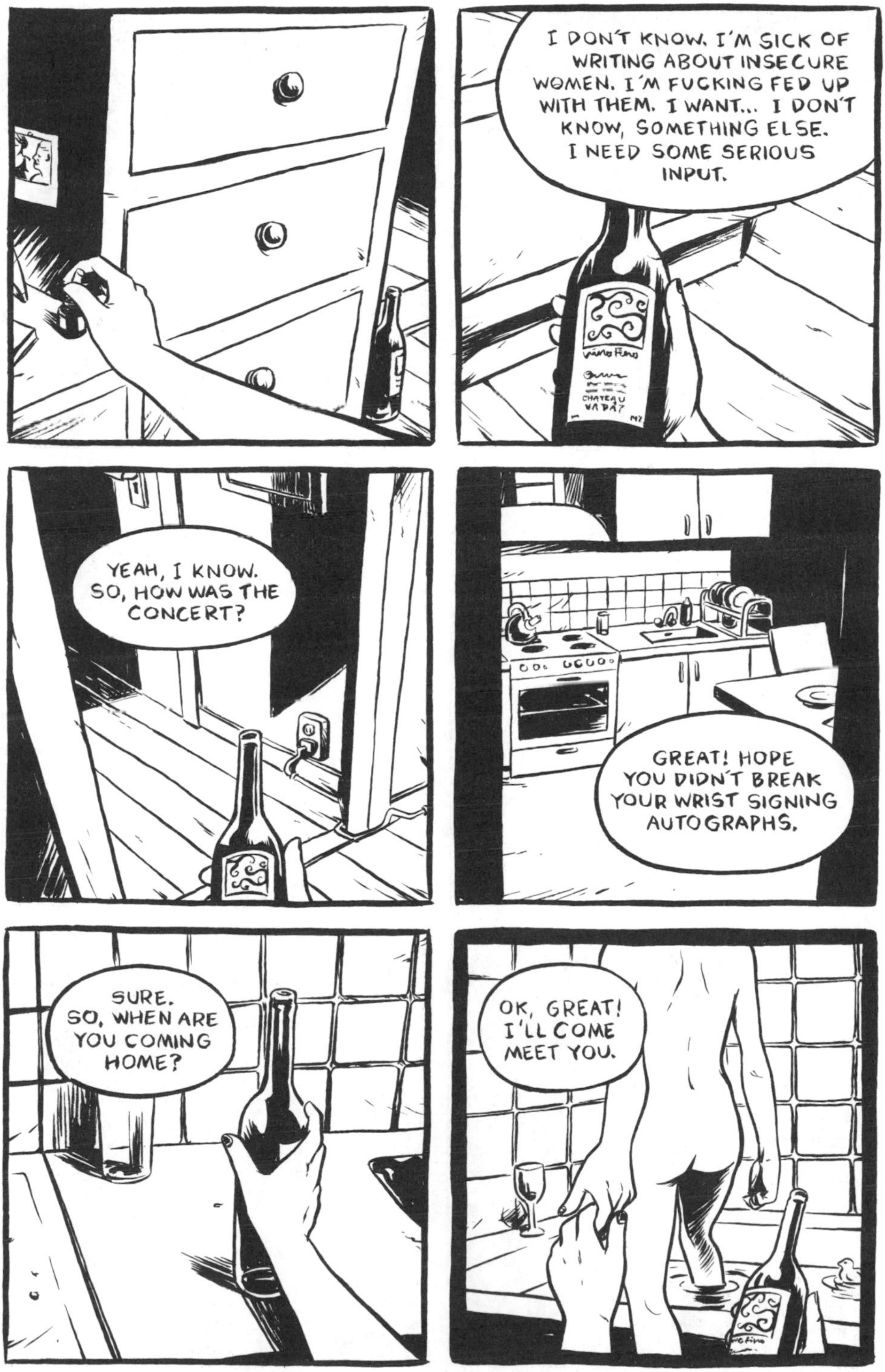
I DON'T KNOW. I'M SICK OF WRITING ABOUT INSECURE WOMEN. I'M FUCKING FED UP WITH THEM. I WANT... I DON'T KNOW, SOMETHING ELSE. I NEED SOME SERIOUS INPUT.
YEAH, I KNOW. SO, HOW WAS THE CONCERT?
GREAT! HOPE YOU DIDN'T BREAK YOUR WRIST SIGNING AUTOGRAPHS.
SURE. SO, WHEN ARE YOU COMING HOME?
OK, GREAT! I'LL COME MEET YOU.

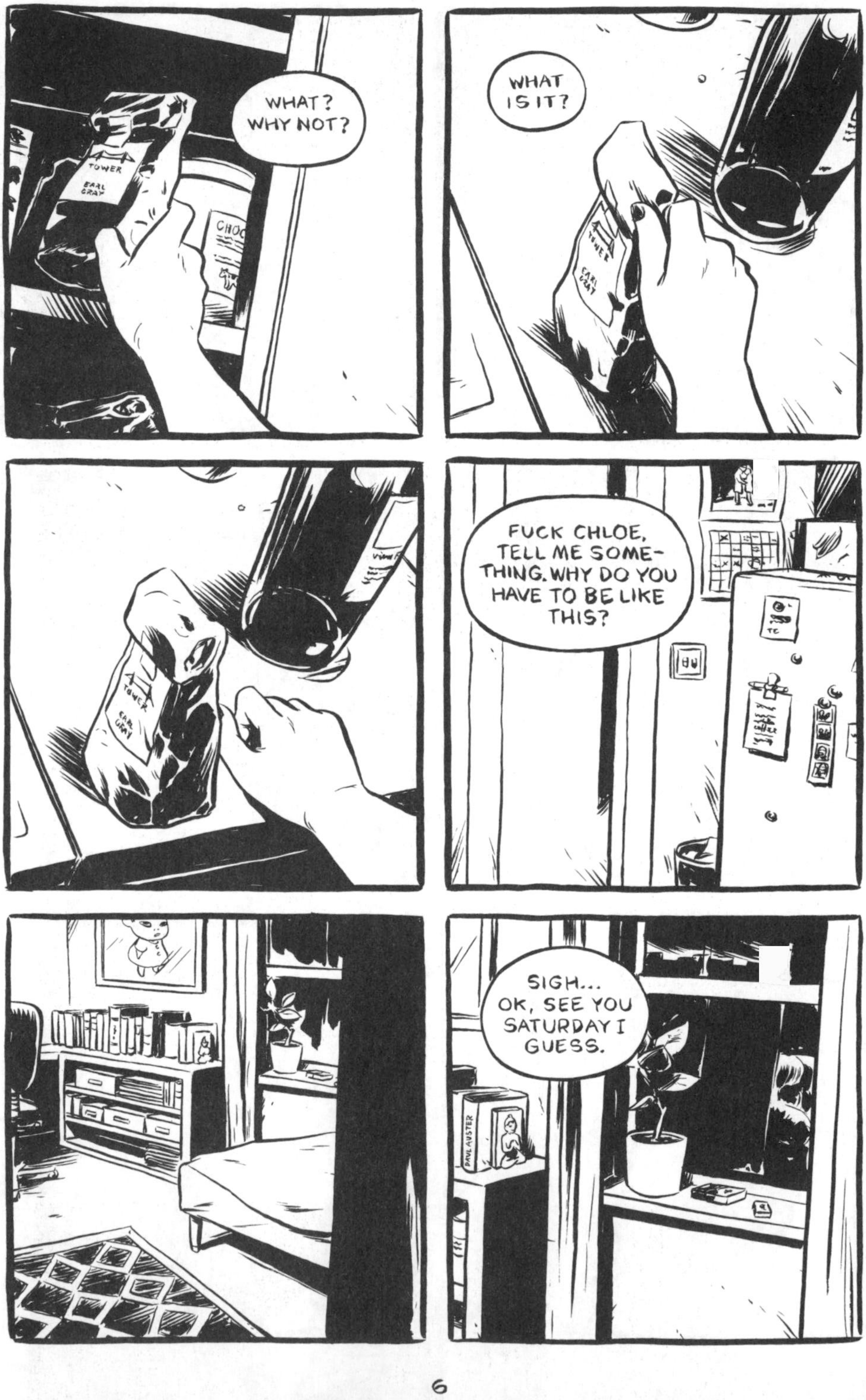
WHAT? WHY NOT?
WHAT IS IT?
FUCK CHLOE, TELL ME SOME-THING. WHY DO YOU HAVE TO BE LIKE THIS?
SIGH... OK, SEE YOU SATURDAY I GUESS.

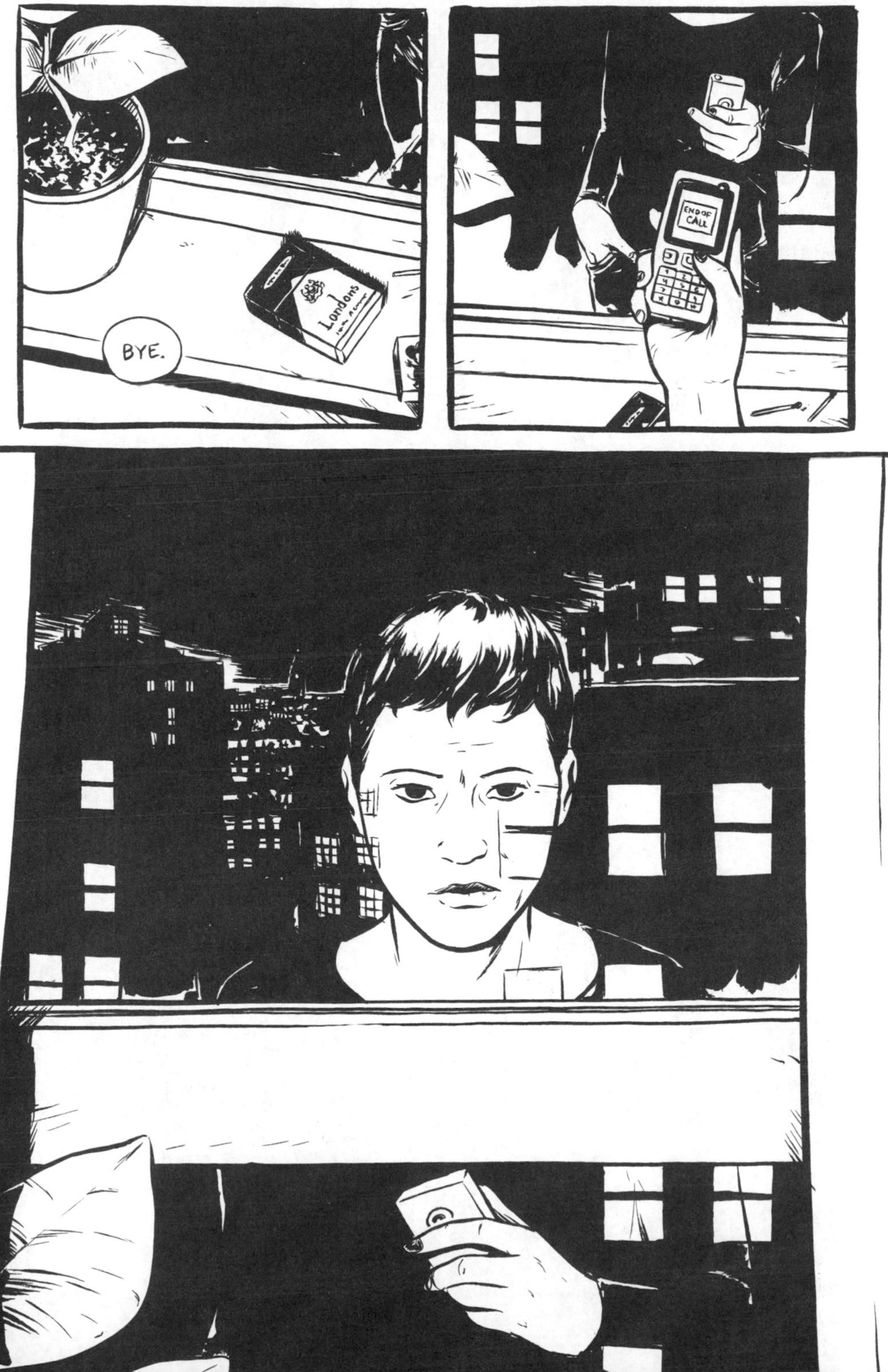
Londons
BYE.
END OF CALL

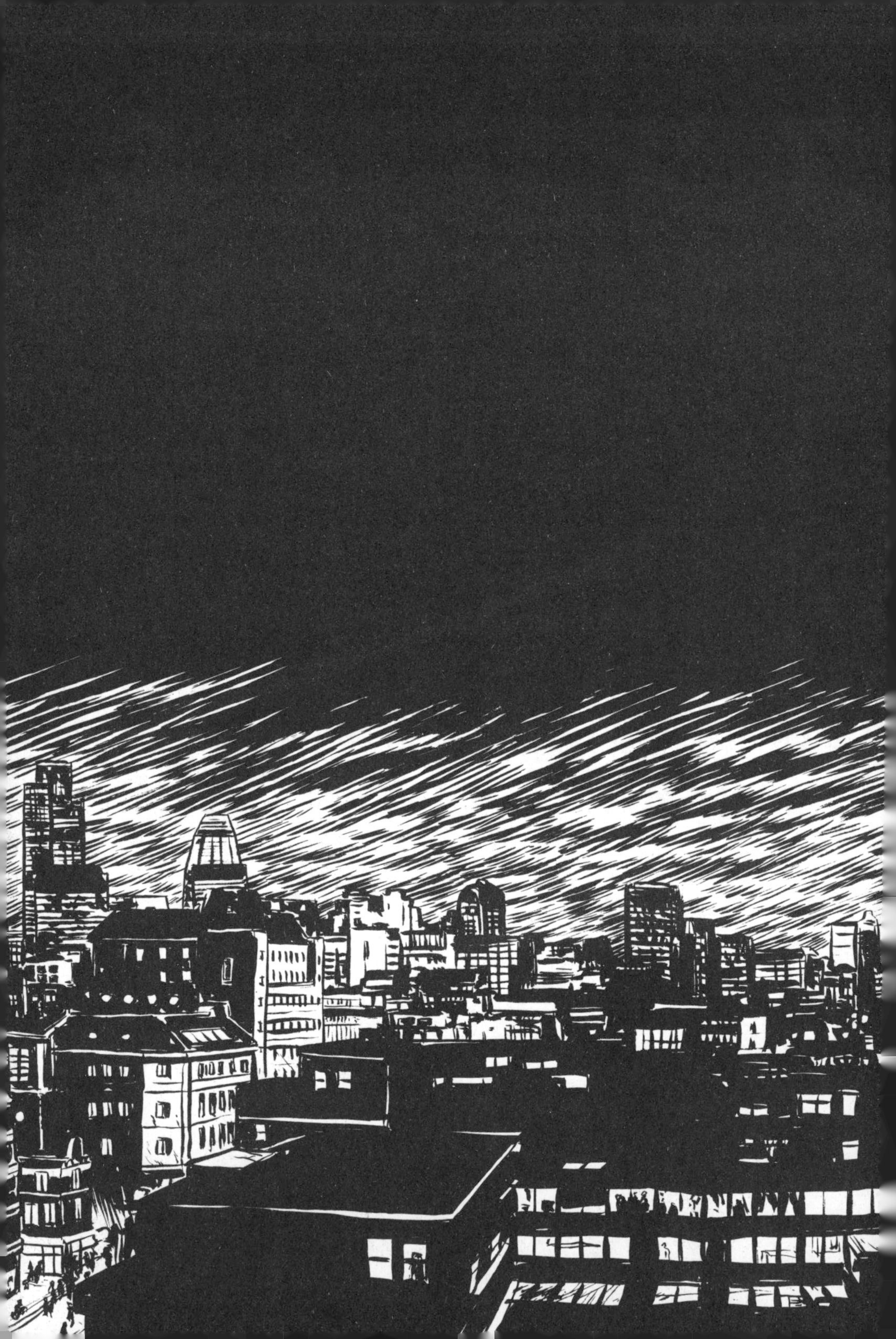

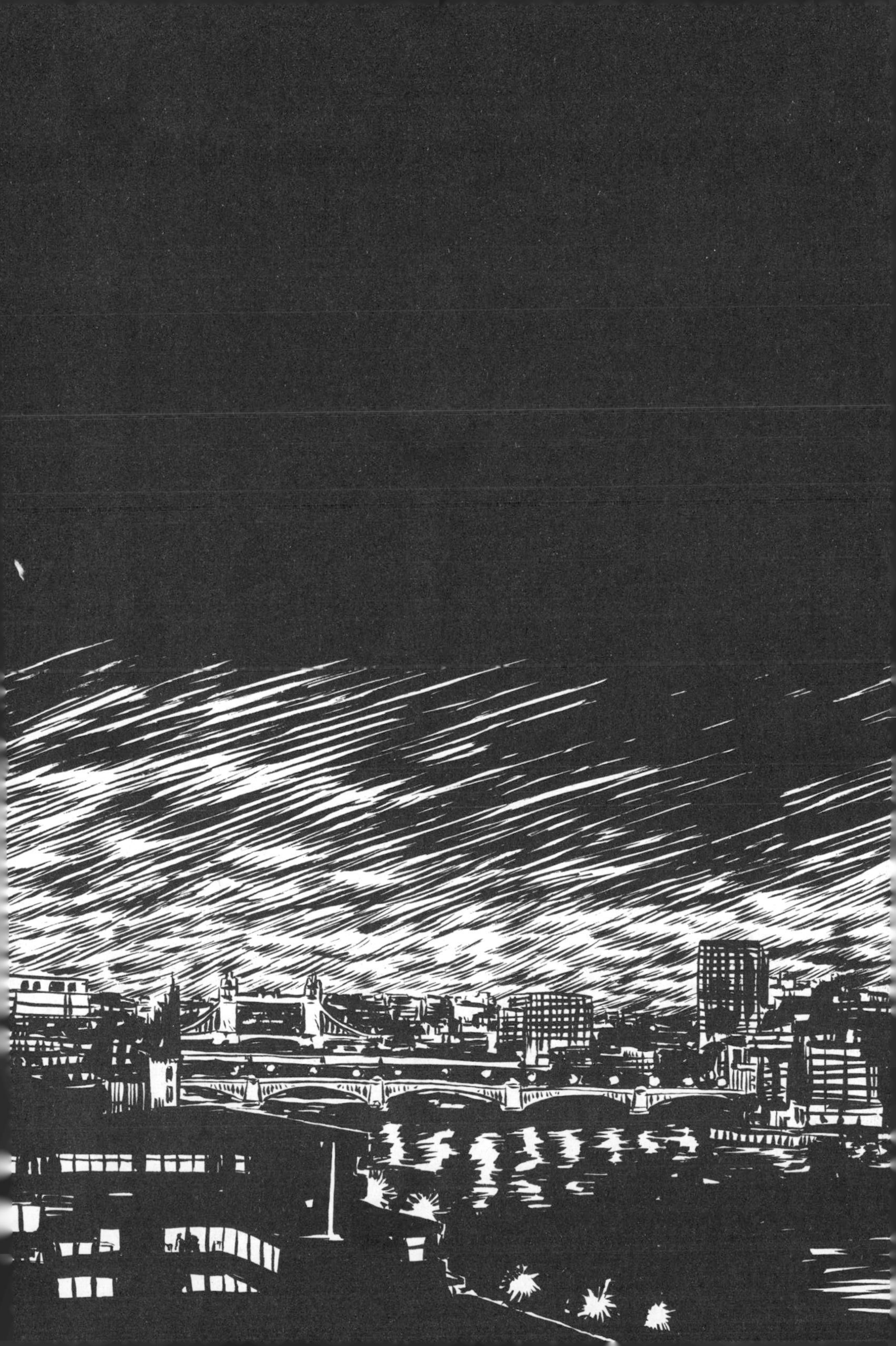

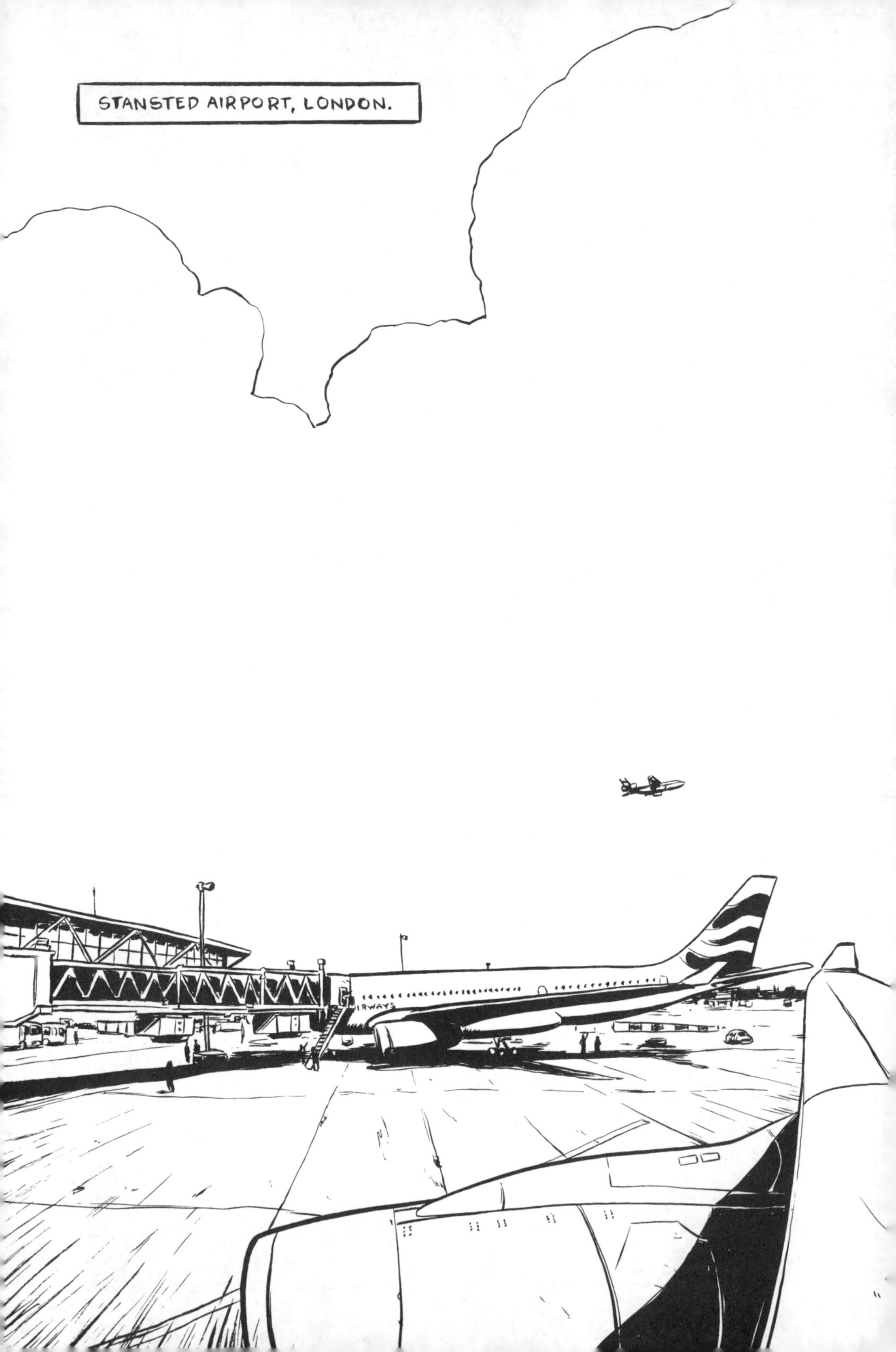
STANSTED AIRPORT, LONDON.

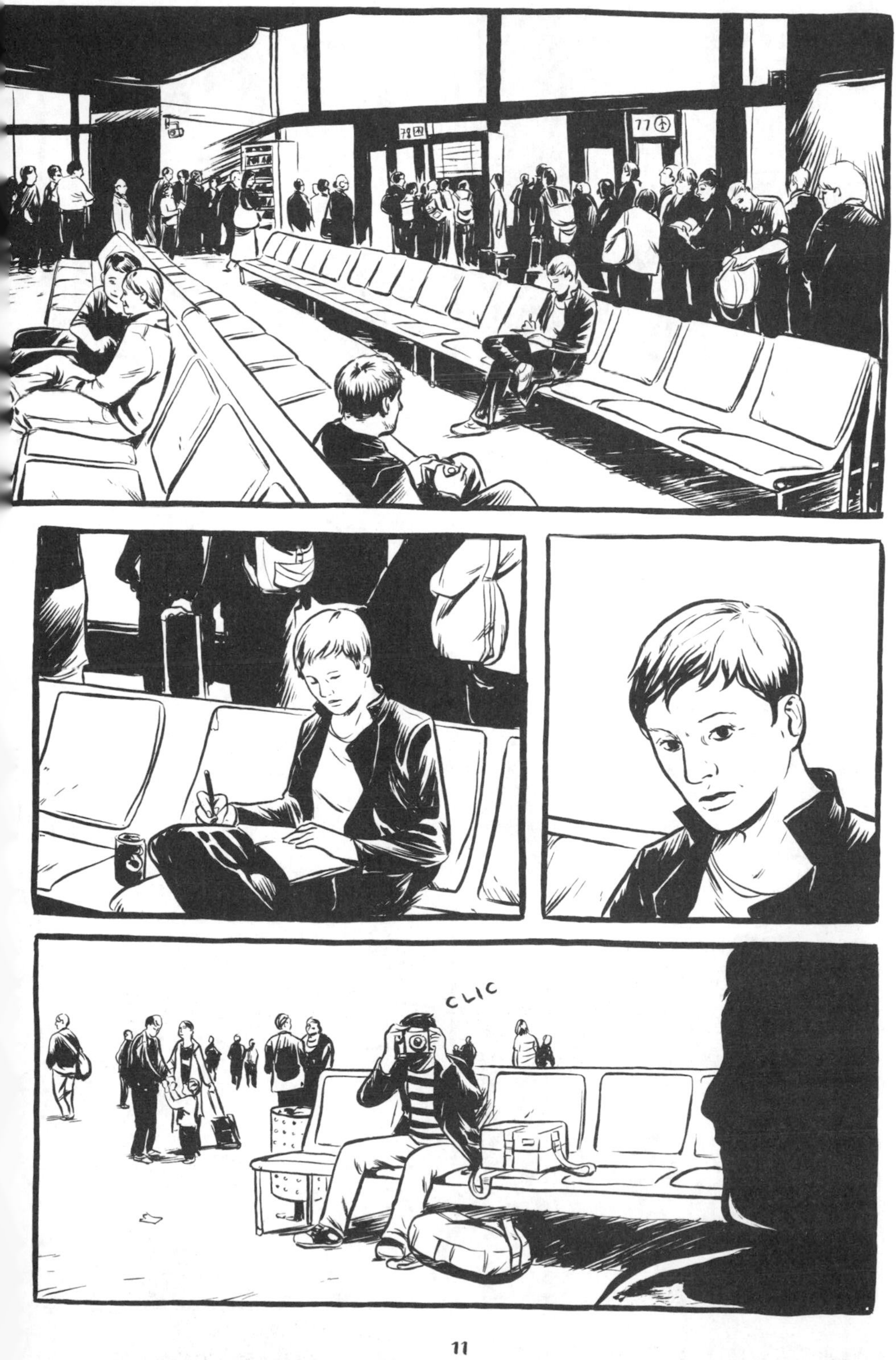
78
77
CLIC

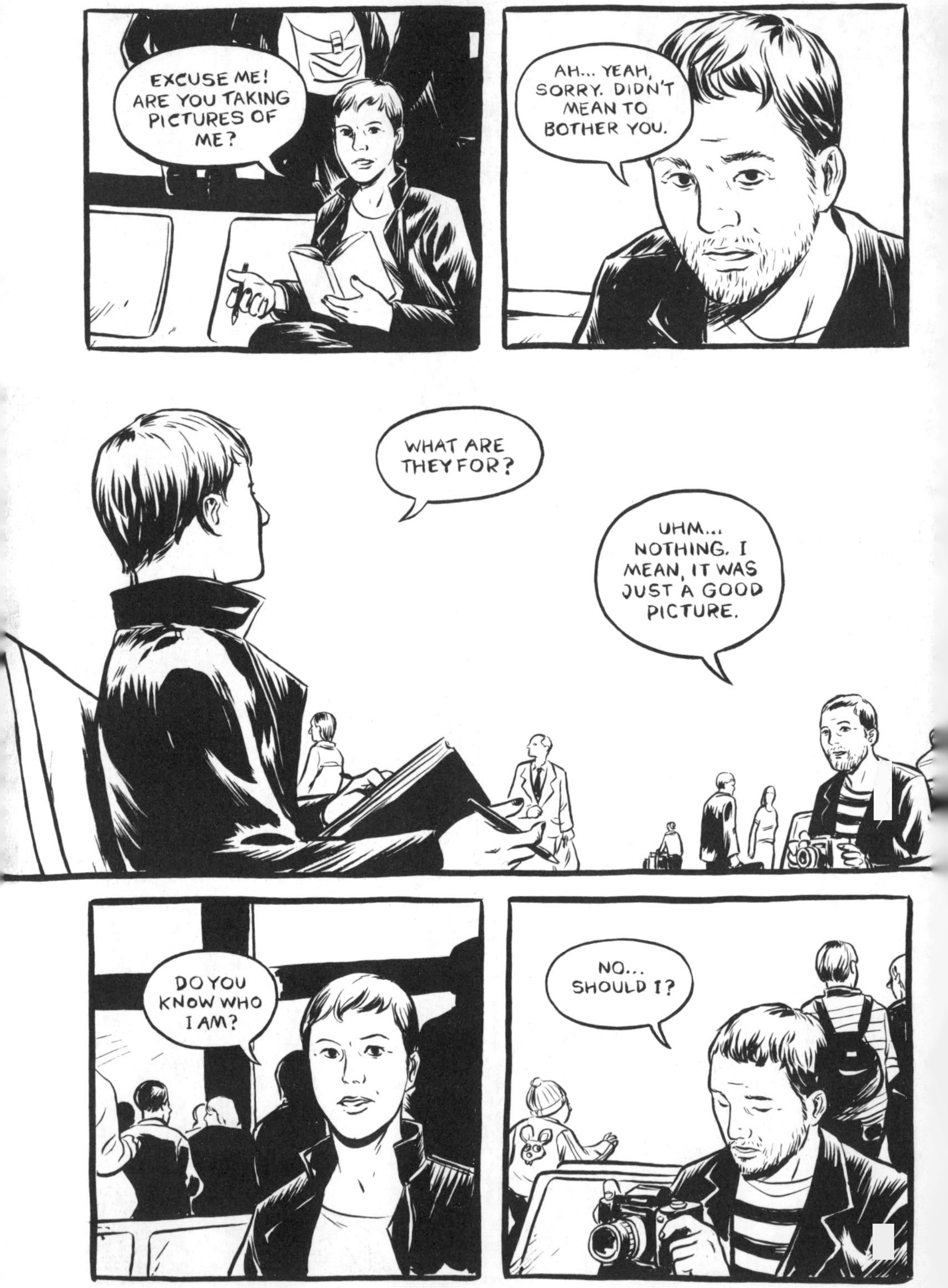
EXCUSE ME! ARE YOU TAKING PICTURES OF ME?
AH... YEAH, SORRY. DIDN'T MEAN TO BOTHER YOU.
WHAT ARE THEY FOR?
UHM... NOTHING. I MEAN, IT WAS JUST A GOOD PICTURE.
DO YOU KNOW WHO I AM?
NO... SHOULD I?

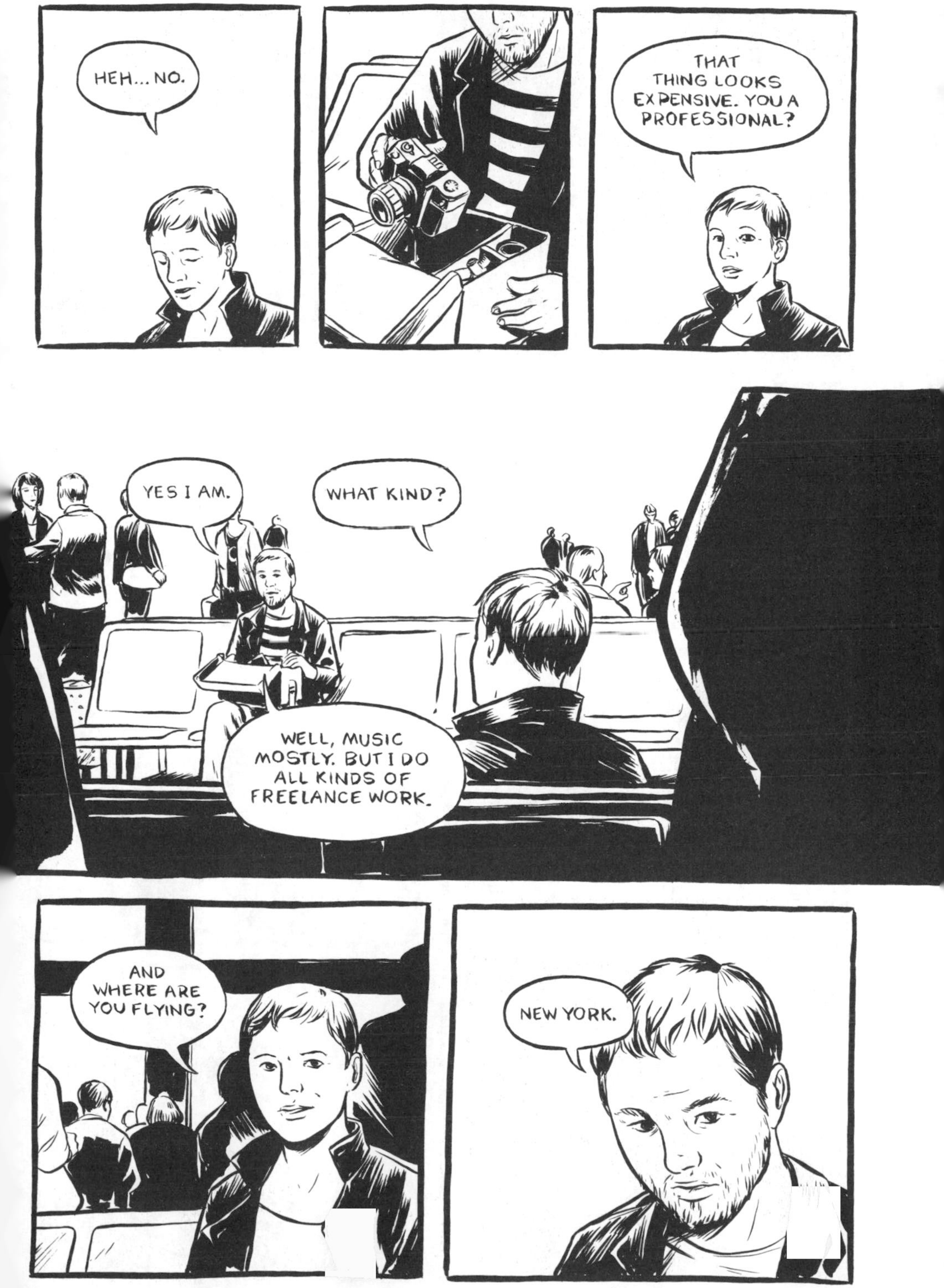
HEH... NO.
THAT THING LOOKS EXPENSIVE. YOU A PROFESSIONAL?
YES I AM.
WHAT KIND?
WELL, MUSIC MOSTLY. BUT I DO ALL KINDS OF FREELANCE WORK.
AND WHERE ARE YOU FLYING?
NEW YORK.

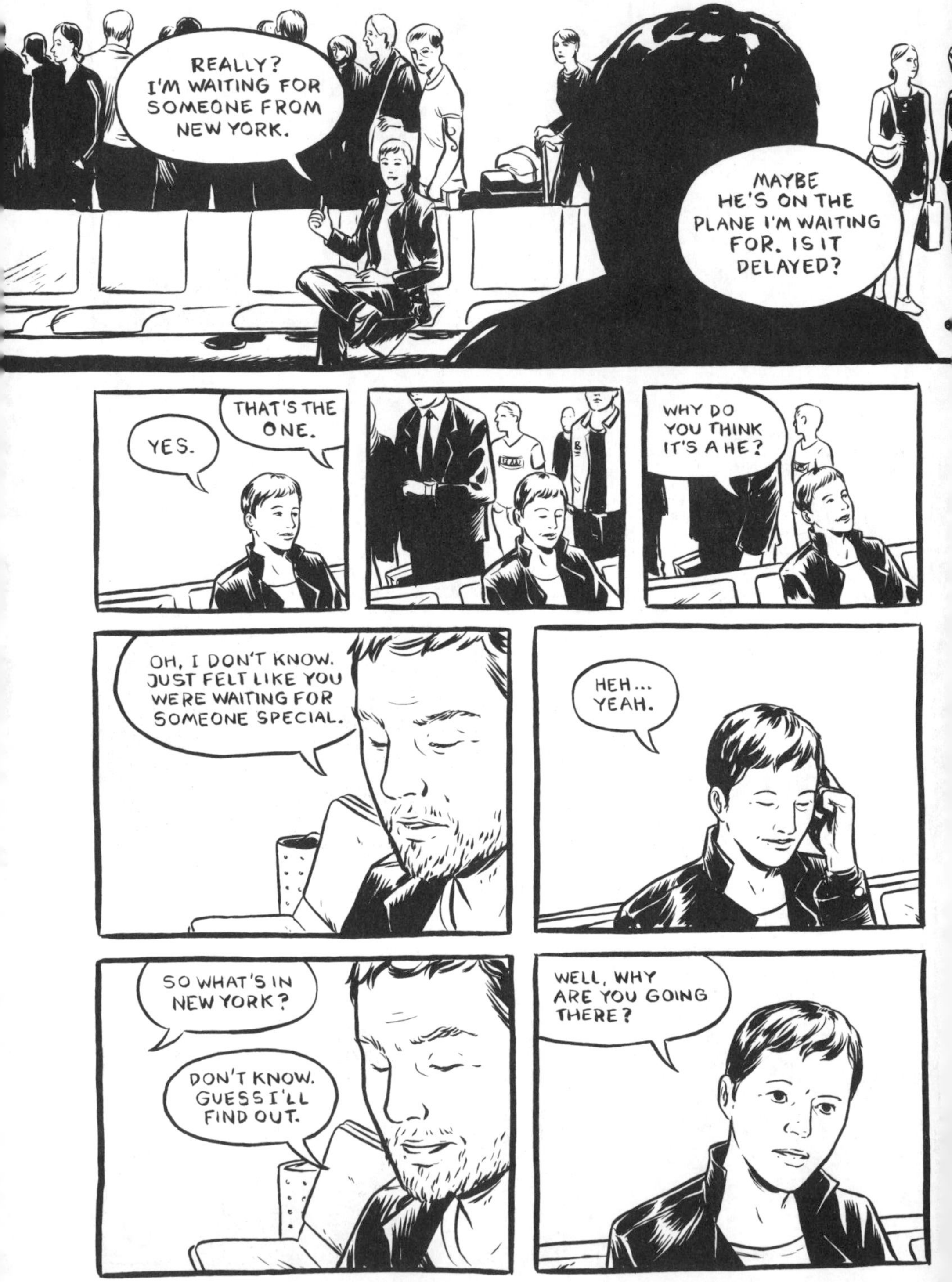
REALLY? I'M WAITING FOR SOMEONE FROM NEW YORK.
MAYBE HE'S ON THE PLANE I'M WAITING FOR. IS IT DELAYED?
YES.
THAT'S THE ONE.
WHY DO YOU THINK IT'S A HE?
OH, I DON'T KNOW. JUST FELT LIKE YOU WERE WAITING FOR SOMEONE SPECIAL.
HEH... YEAH.
SO WHAT'S IN NEW YORK?
DON'T KNOW. GUESS I'LL FIND OUT.
WELL, WHY ARE YOU GOING THERE?

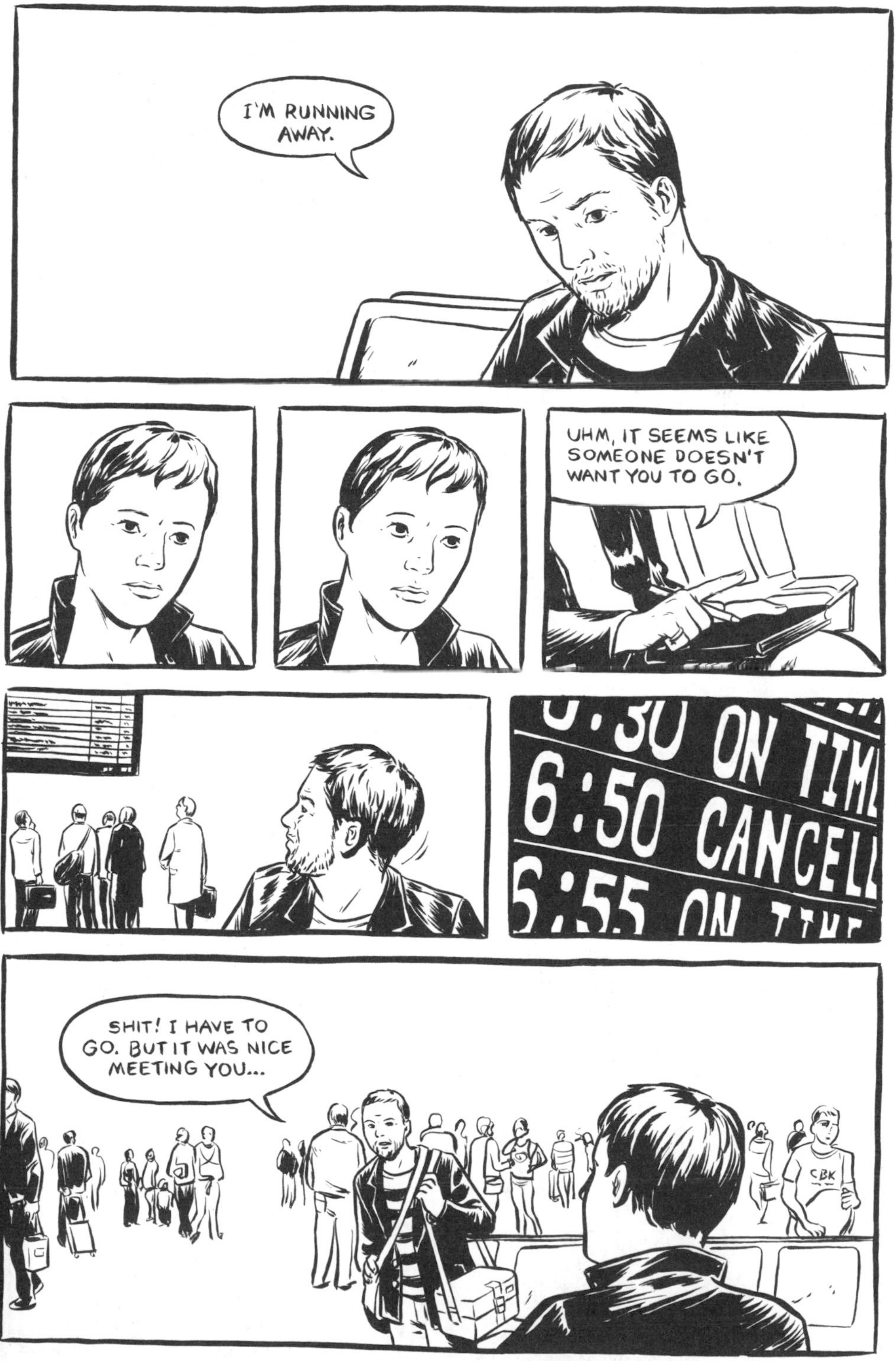
I'M RUNNING AWAY.
UHM, IT SEEMS LIKE SOMEONE DOESN'T WANT YOU TO GO.
ON TIM
6:50 CANCELL
SHIT! I HAVE TO GO. BUT IT WAS NICE MEETING YOU...
CBK

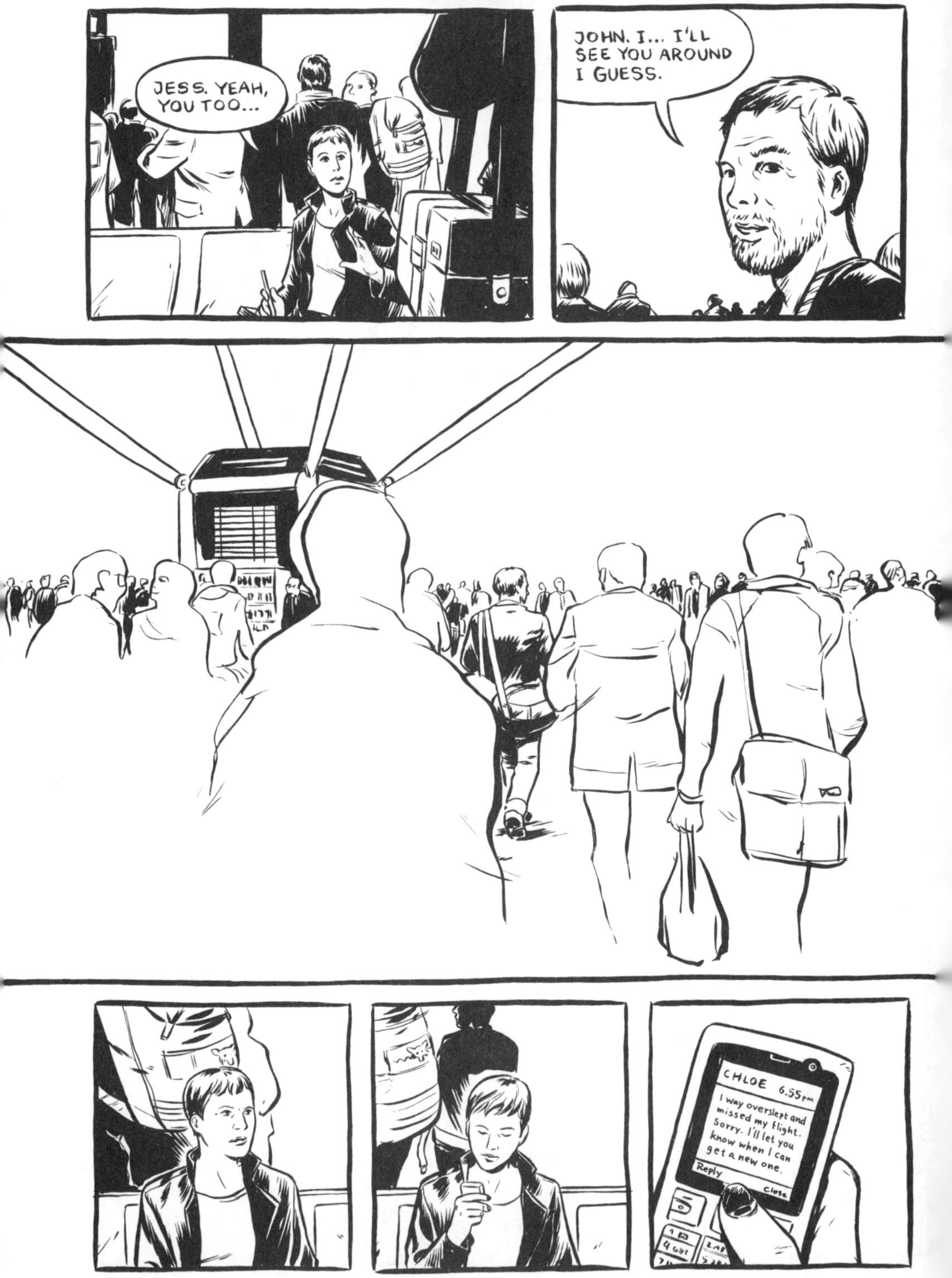
JESS. YEAH, YOU TOO...
JOHN. I... I'LL SEE YOU AROUND I GUESS.
CHLOE 6.55pm
I way overslept and missed my flight. Sorry. I'll let you know when I can get a new one.
Reply
Close

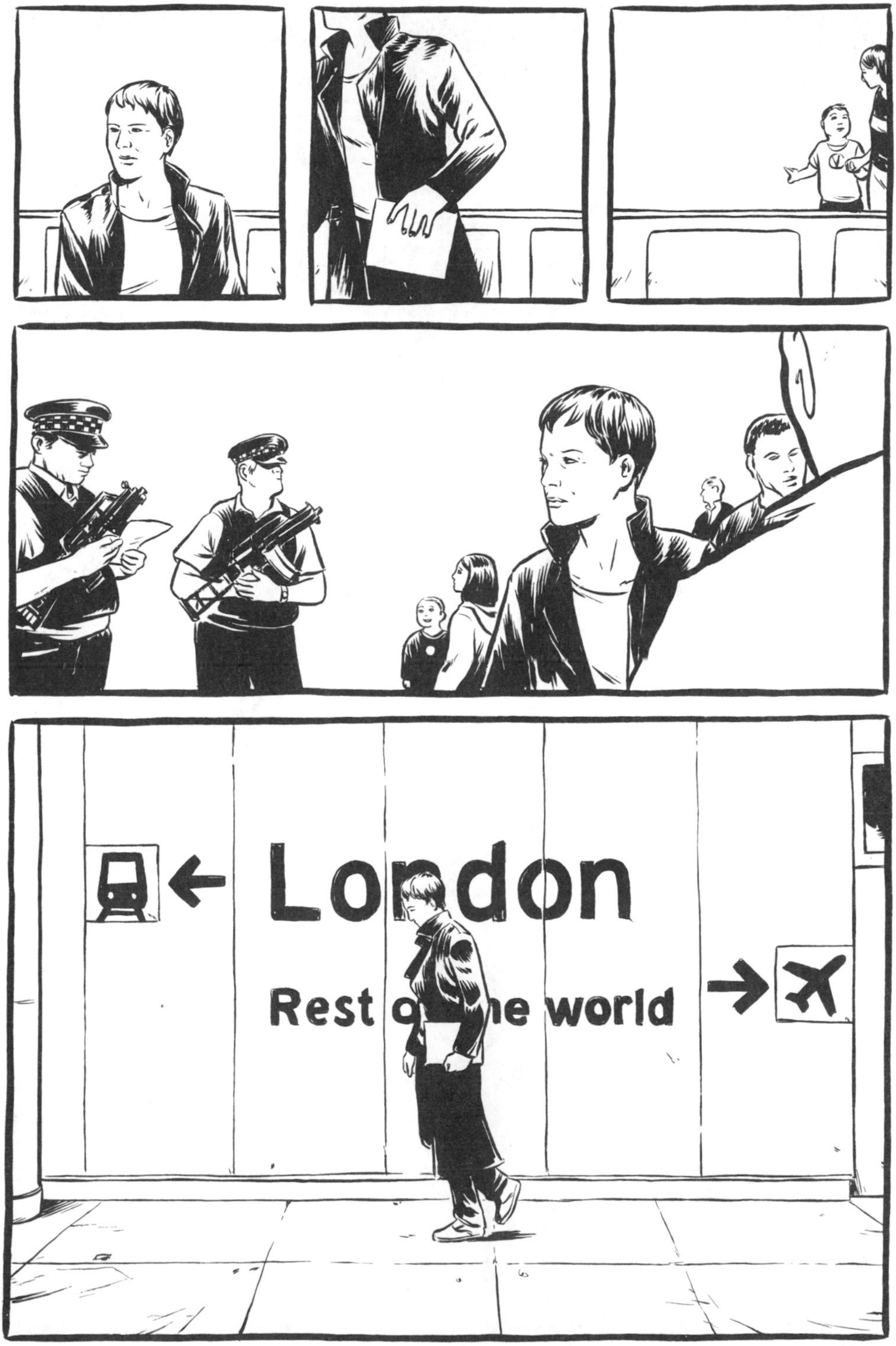
London
Rest o he world

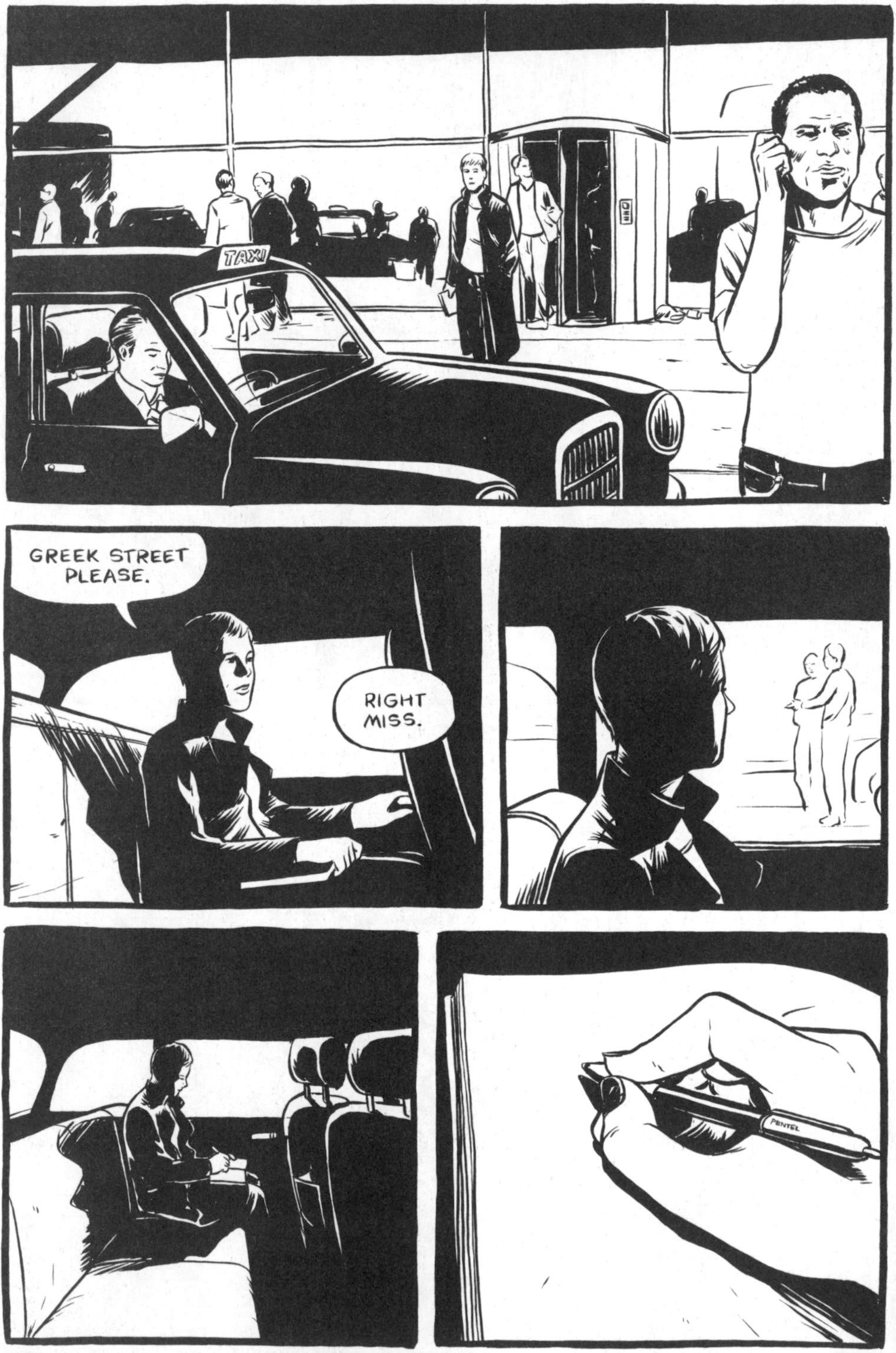
TAXI
GREEK STREET PLEASE.
RIGHT MISS.
PENTEL

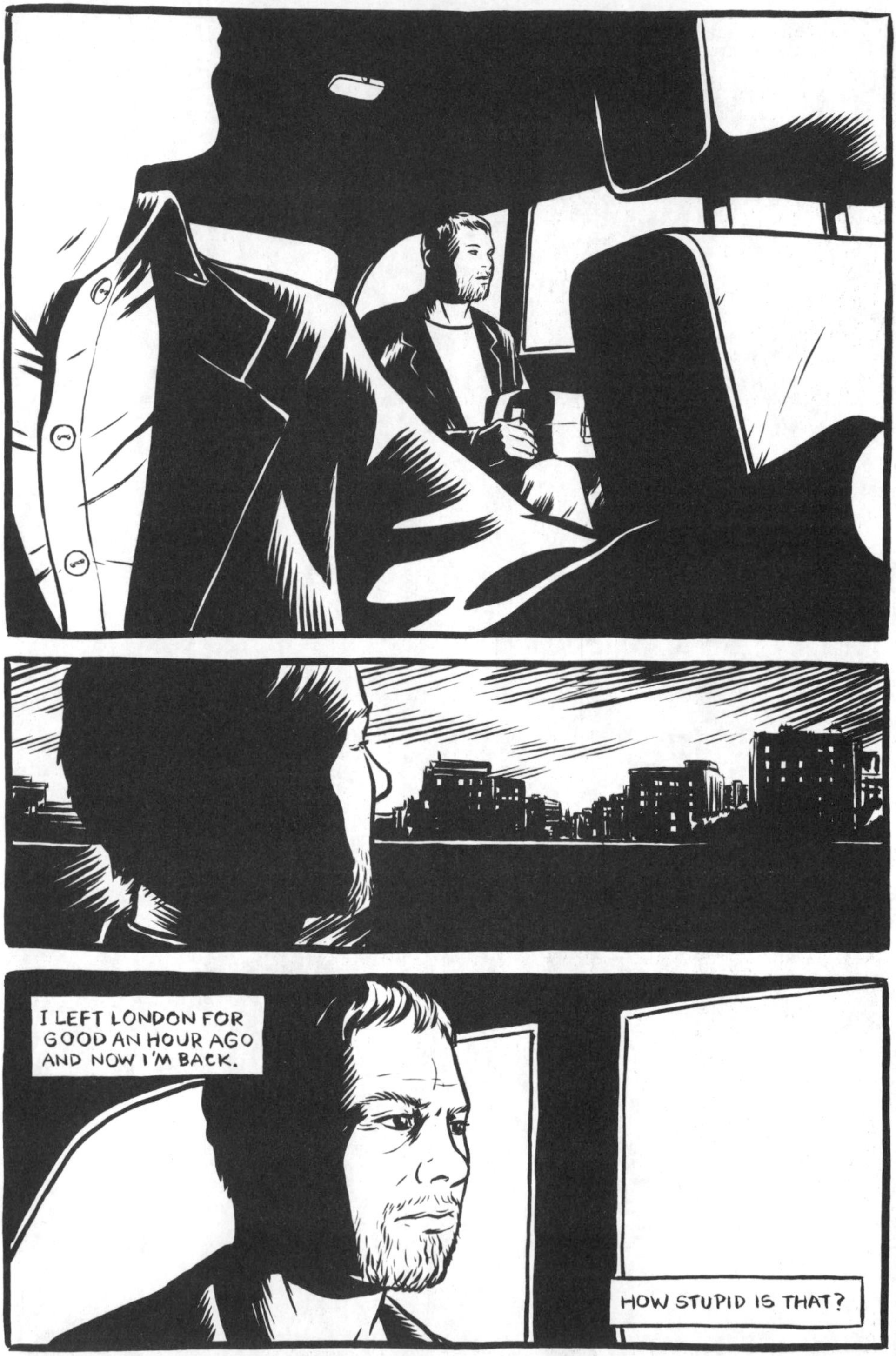
I LEFT LONDON FOR GOOD AN HOUR AGO AND NOW I'M BACK.
HOW STUPID IS THAT?

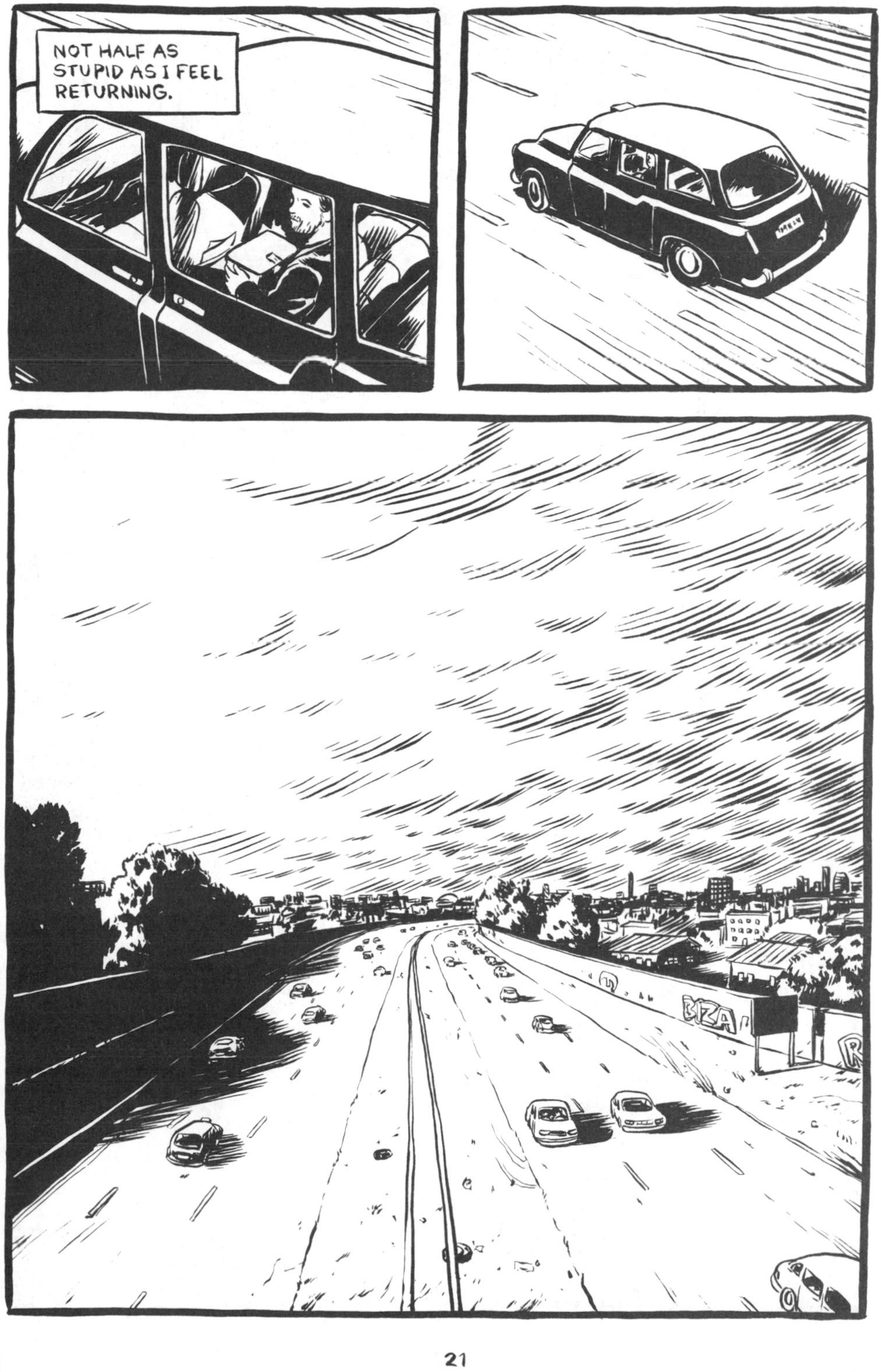
NOT HALF AS STUPID AS I FEEL RETURNING.
BIZA

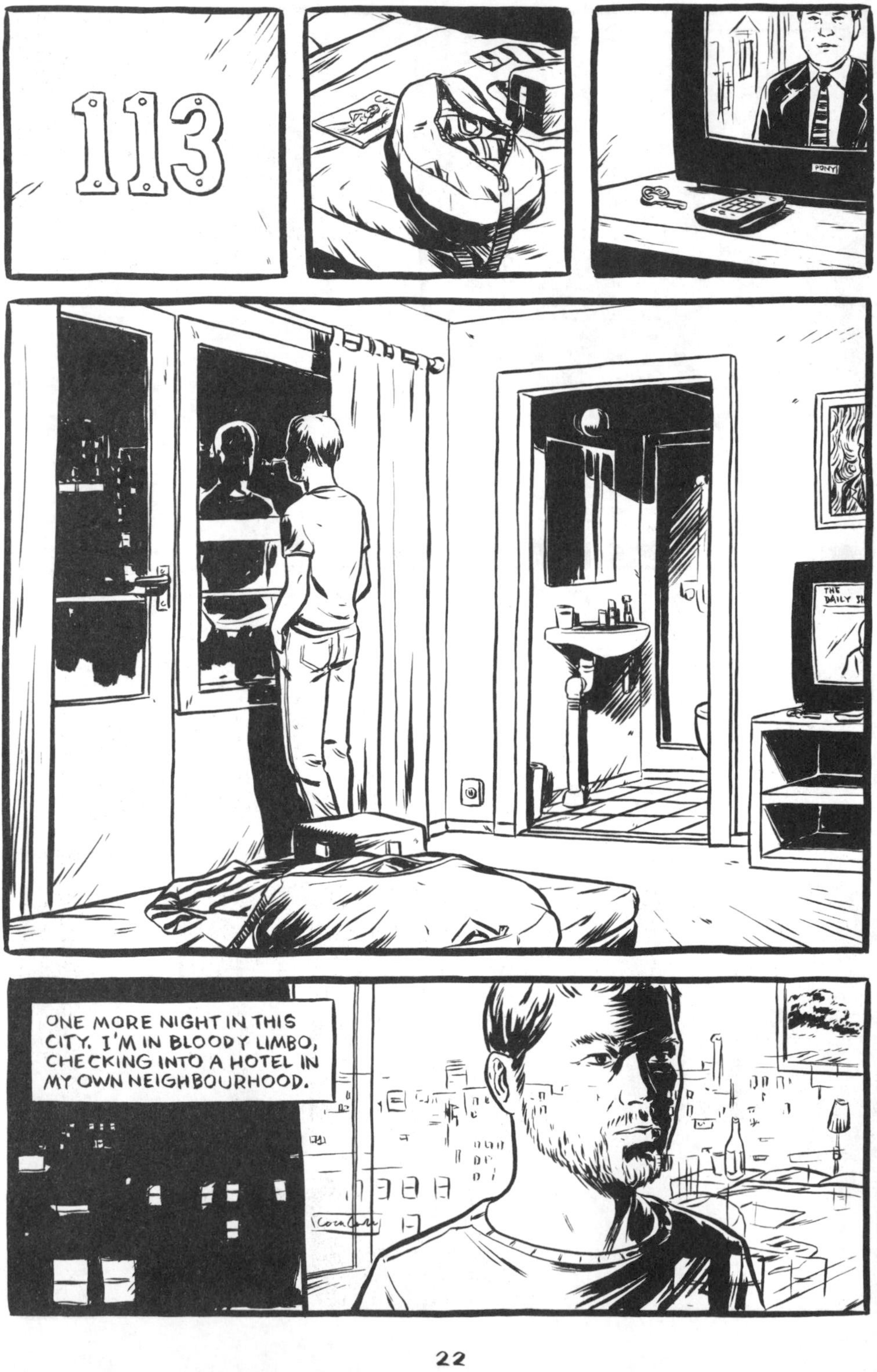
113
PONY
ONE MORE NIGHT IN THIS CITY. I'M IN BLOODY LIMBO, CHECKING INTO A HOTEL IN MY OWN NEIGHBOURHOOD.

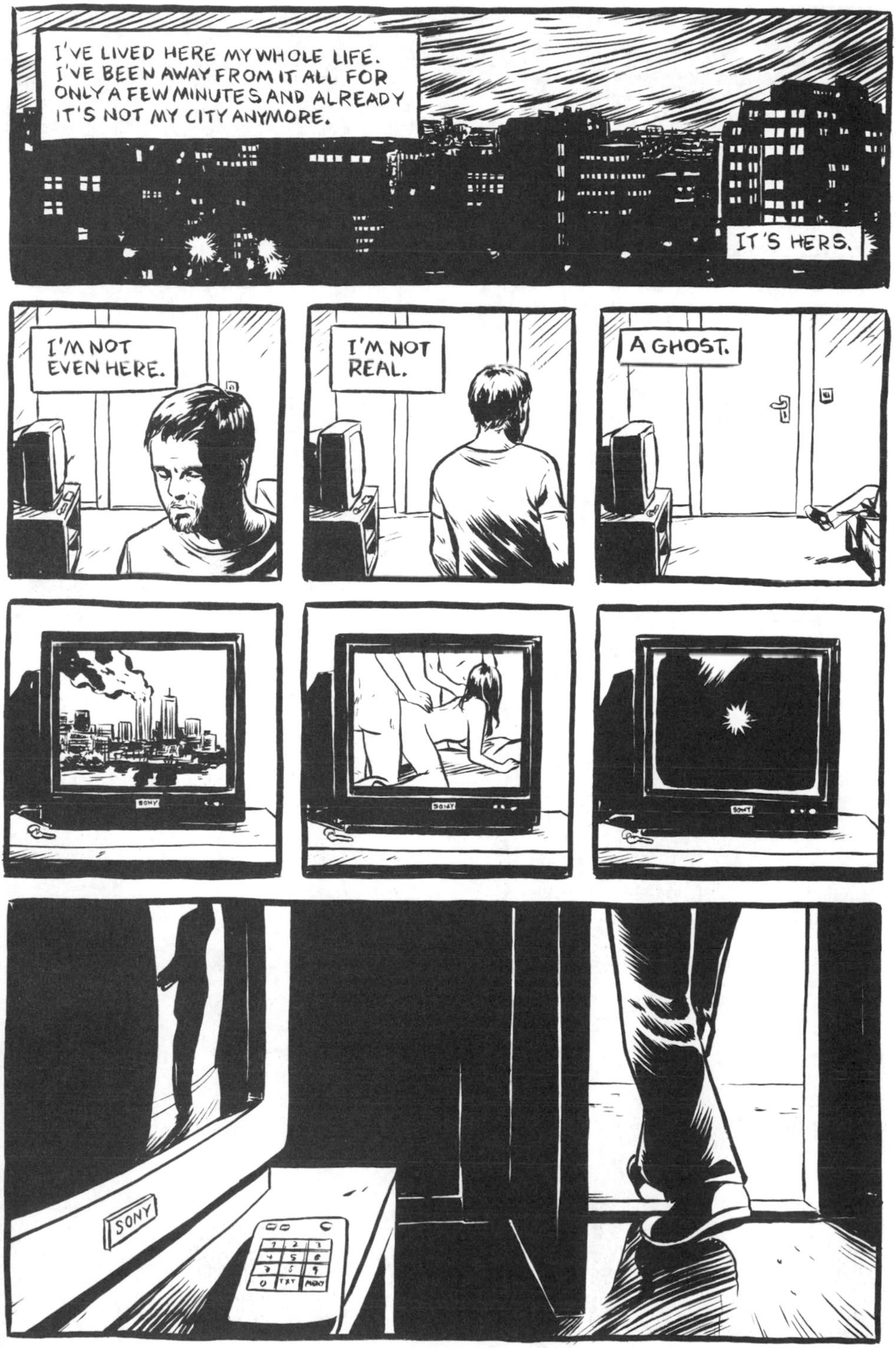
I'VE LIVED HERE MY WHOLE LIFE. I'VE BEEN AWAY FROM IT ALL FOR ONLY A FEW MINUTES AND ALREADY IT'S NOT MY CITY ANYMORE.
IT'S HERS.
I'M NOT EVEN HERE.
I'M NOT REAL.
A GHOST.
SONY
SONY
SONY
SONY

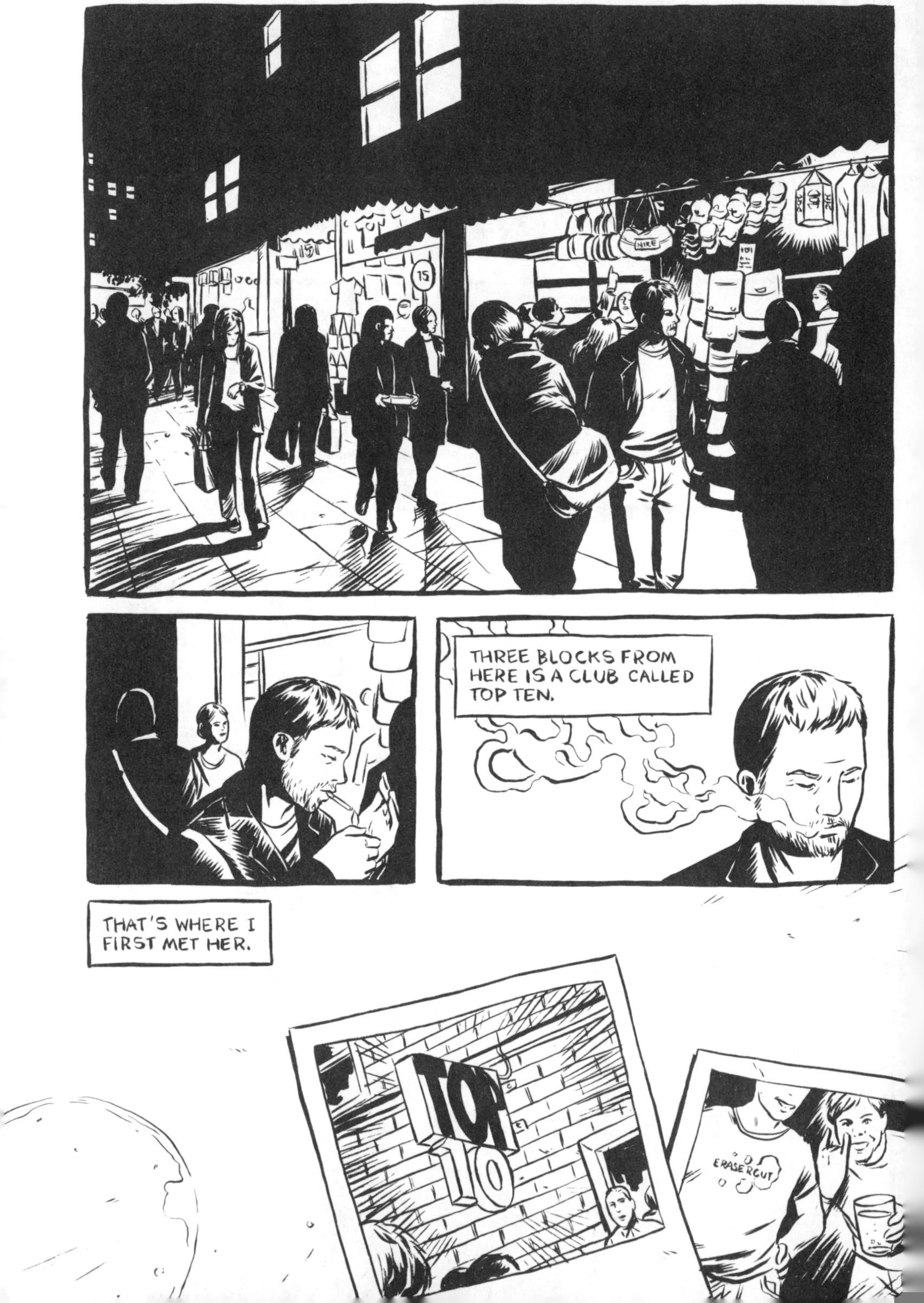
15
NIKE
THREE BLOCKS FROM HERE IS A CLUB CALLED TOP TEN.
THAT'S WHERE I FIRST MET HER.
TOP
10
ERASERCUT

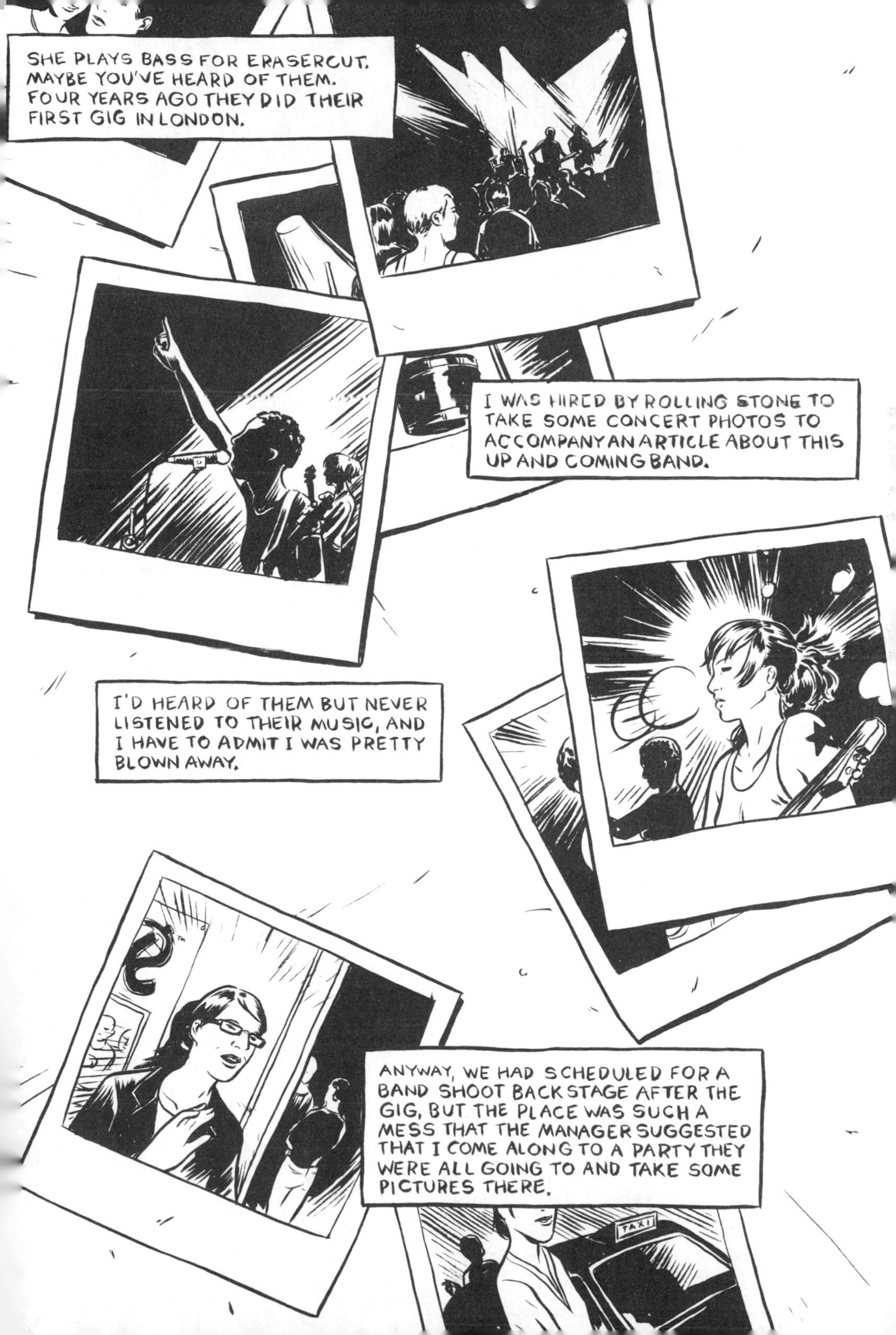
SHE PLAYS BASS FOR ERASERCUT. MAYBE YOU'VE HEARD OF THEM. FOUR YEARS AGO THEY DID THEIR FIRST GIG IN LONDON.
I WAS HIRED BY ROLLING STONE TO TAKE SOME CONCERT PHOTOS TO ACCOMPANY AN ARTICLE ABOUT THIS UP AND COMING BAND.
I'D HEARD OF THEM BUT NEVER LISTENED TO THEIR MUSIC, AND I HAVE TO ADMIT I WAS PRETTY BLOWN AWAY.
ANYWAY, WE HAD SCHEDULED FOR A BAND SHOOT BACKSTAGE AFTER THE GIG, BUT THE PLACE WAS SUCH A MESS THAT THE MANAGER SUGGESTED THAT I COME ALONG TO A PARTY THEY WERE ALL GOING TO AND TAKE SOME PICTURES THERE.
TAXI

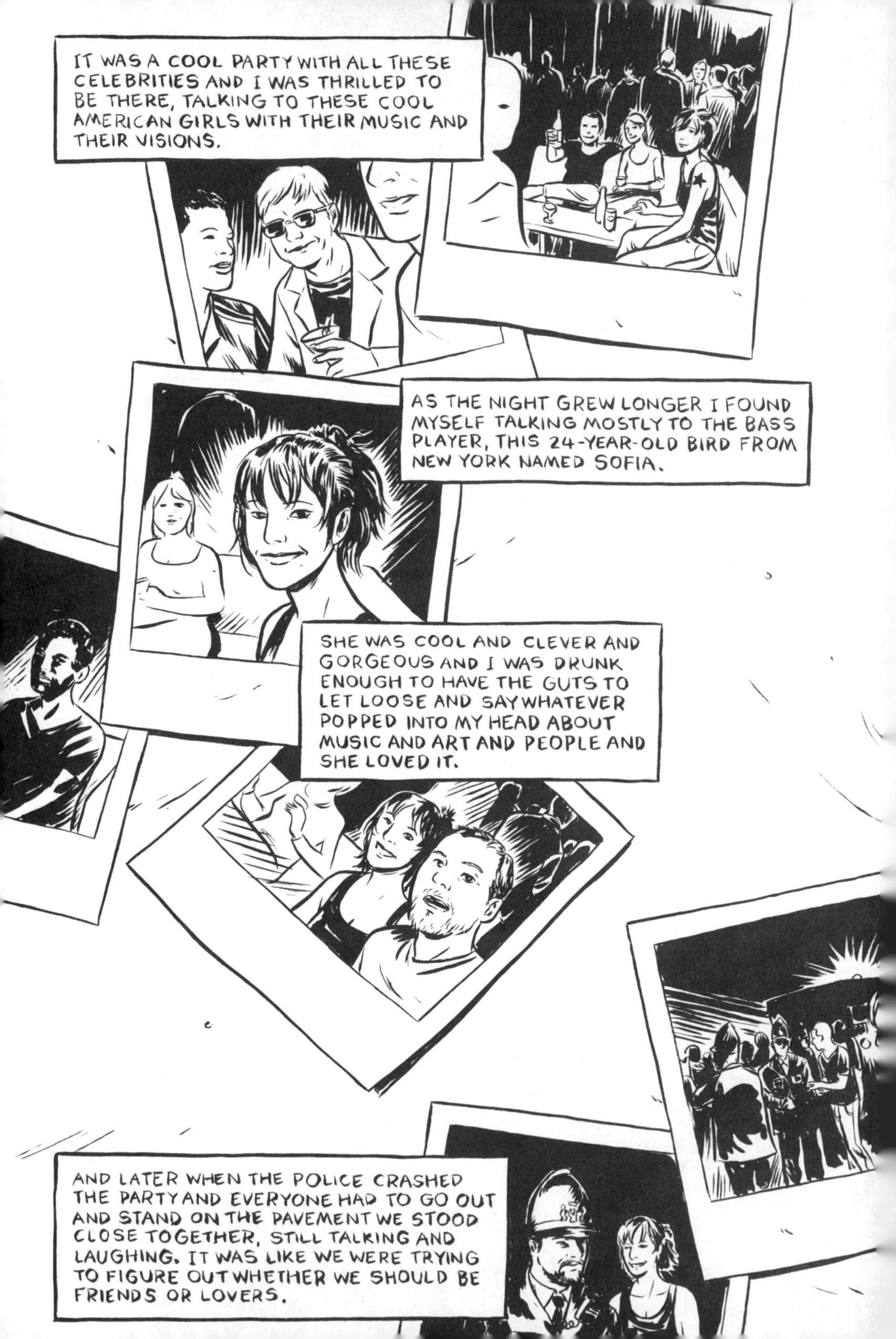
IT WAS A COOL PARTY WITH ALL THESE CELEBRITIES AND I WAS THRILLED TO BE THERE, TALKING TO THESE COOL AMERICAN GIRLS WITH THEIR MUSIC AND THEIR VISIONS.
AS THE NIGHT GREW LONGER I FOUND MYSELF TALKING MOSTLY TO THE BASS PLAYER, THIS 24-YEAR-OLD BIRD FROM NEW YORK NAMED SOFIA.
SHE WAS COOL AND CLEVER AND GORGEOUS AND I WAS DRUNK ENOUGH TO HAVE THE GUTS TO LET LOOSE AND SAY WHATEVER POPPED INTO MY HEAD ABOUT MUSIC AND ART AND PEOPLE AND SHE LOVED IT.
AND LATER WHEN THE POLICE CRASHED THE PARTY AND EVERYONE HAD TO GO OUT AND STAND ON THE PAVEMENT WE STOOD CLOSE TOGETHER, STILL TALKING AND LAUGHING. IT WAS LIKE WE WERE TRYING TO FIGURE OUT WHETHER WE SHOULD BE FRIENDS OR LOVERS.

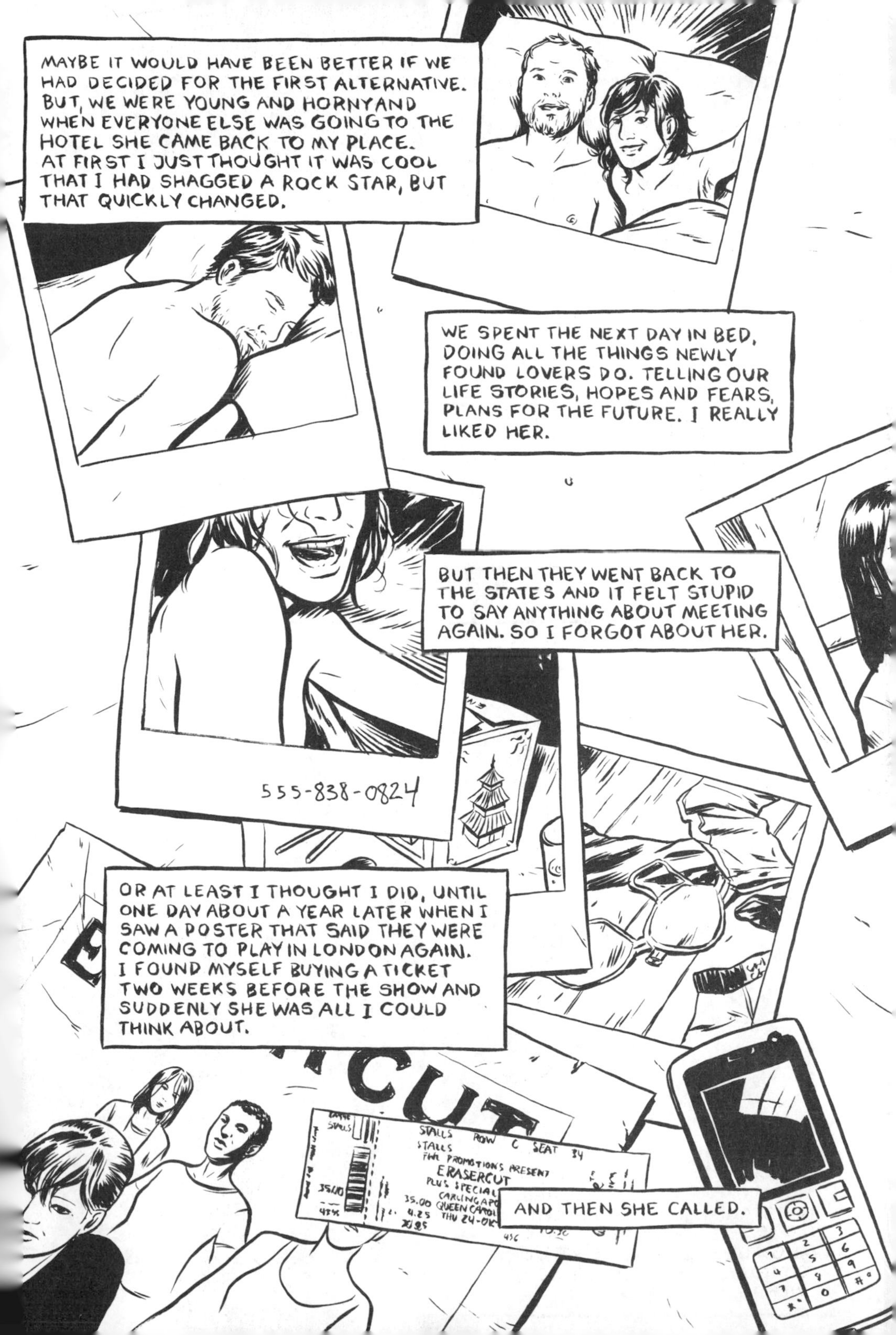
MAYBE IT WOULD HAVE BEEN BETTER IF WE HAD DECIDED FOR THE FIRST ALTERNATIVE. BUT, WE WERE YOUNG AND HORNY AND WHEN EVERYONE ELSE WAS GOING TO THE HOTEL SHE CAME BACK TO MY PLACE. AT FIRST I JUST THOUGHT IT WAS COOL THAT I HAD SHAGGED A ROCK STAR, BUT THAT QUICKLY CHANGED.
WE SPENT THE NEXT DAY IN BED, DOING ALL THE THINGS NEWLY FOUND LOVERS DO. TELLING OUR LIFE STORIES, HOPES AND FEARS, PLANS FOR THE FUTURE. I REALLY LIKED HER.
BUT THEN THEY WENT BACK TO THE STATES AND IT FELT STUPID TO SAY ANYTHING ABOUT MEETING AGAIN. SO I FORGOT ABOUT HER.
555-838-0824
OR AT LEAST I THOUGHT I DID, UNTIL ONE DAY ABOUT A YEAR LATER WHEN I SAW A POSTER THAT SAID THEY WERE COMING TO PLAY IN LONDON AGAIN. I FOUND MYSELF BUYING A TICKET TWO WEEKS BEFORE THE SHOW AND SUDDENLY SHE WAS ALL I COULD THINK ABOUT.
CUT
STALLS ROW C SEAT 34
ERASERCUT
AND THEN SHE CALLED.

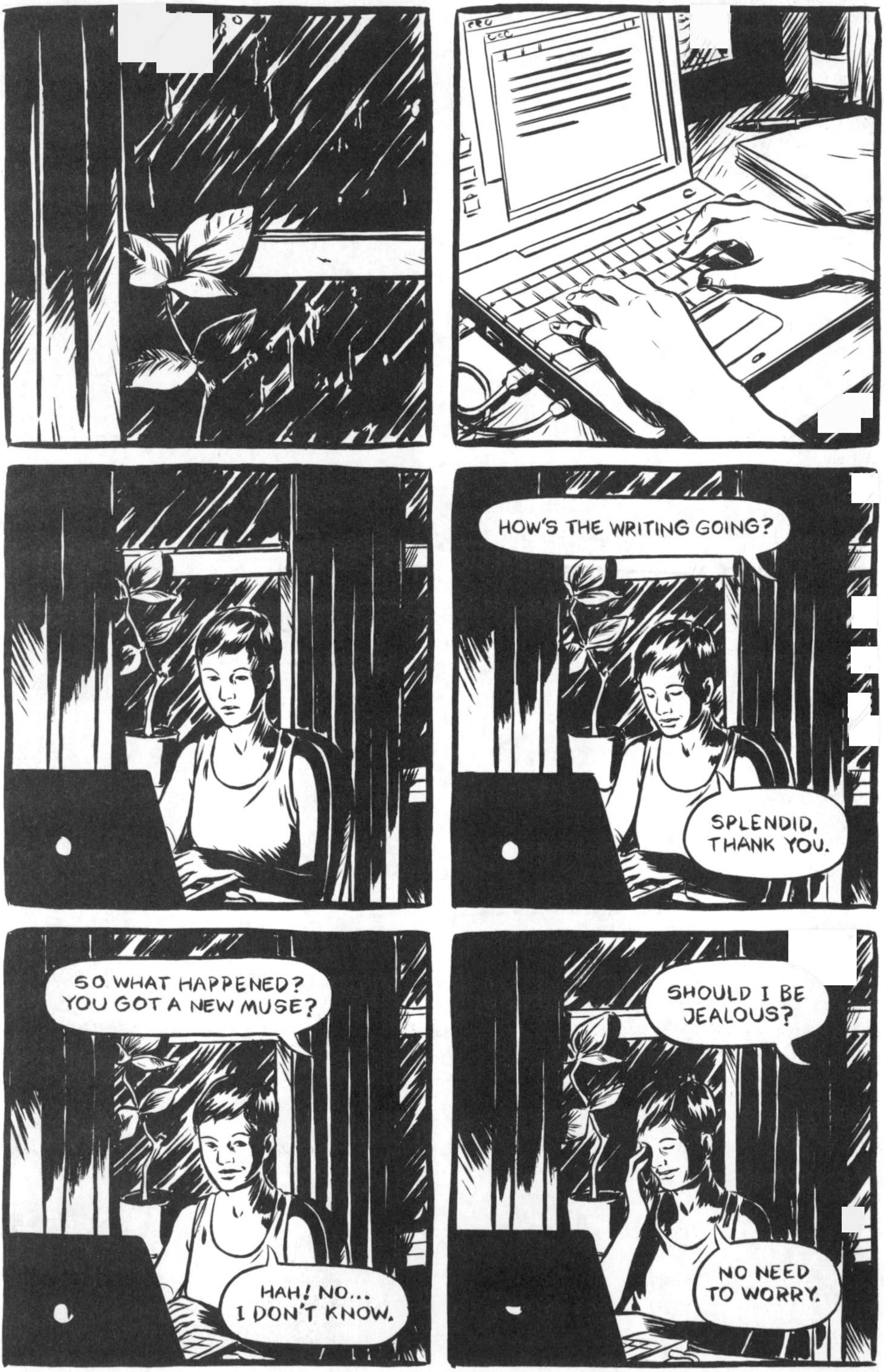
HOW'S THE WRITING GOING?
SPLENDID, THANK YOU.
SO WHAT HAPPENED? YOU GOT A NEW MUSE?
HAH! NO... I DON'T KNOW.
SHOULD I BE JEALOUS?
NO NEED TO WORRY.

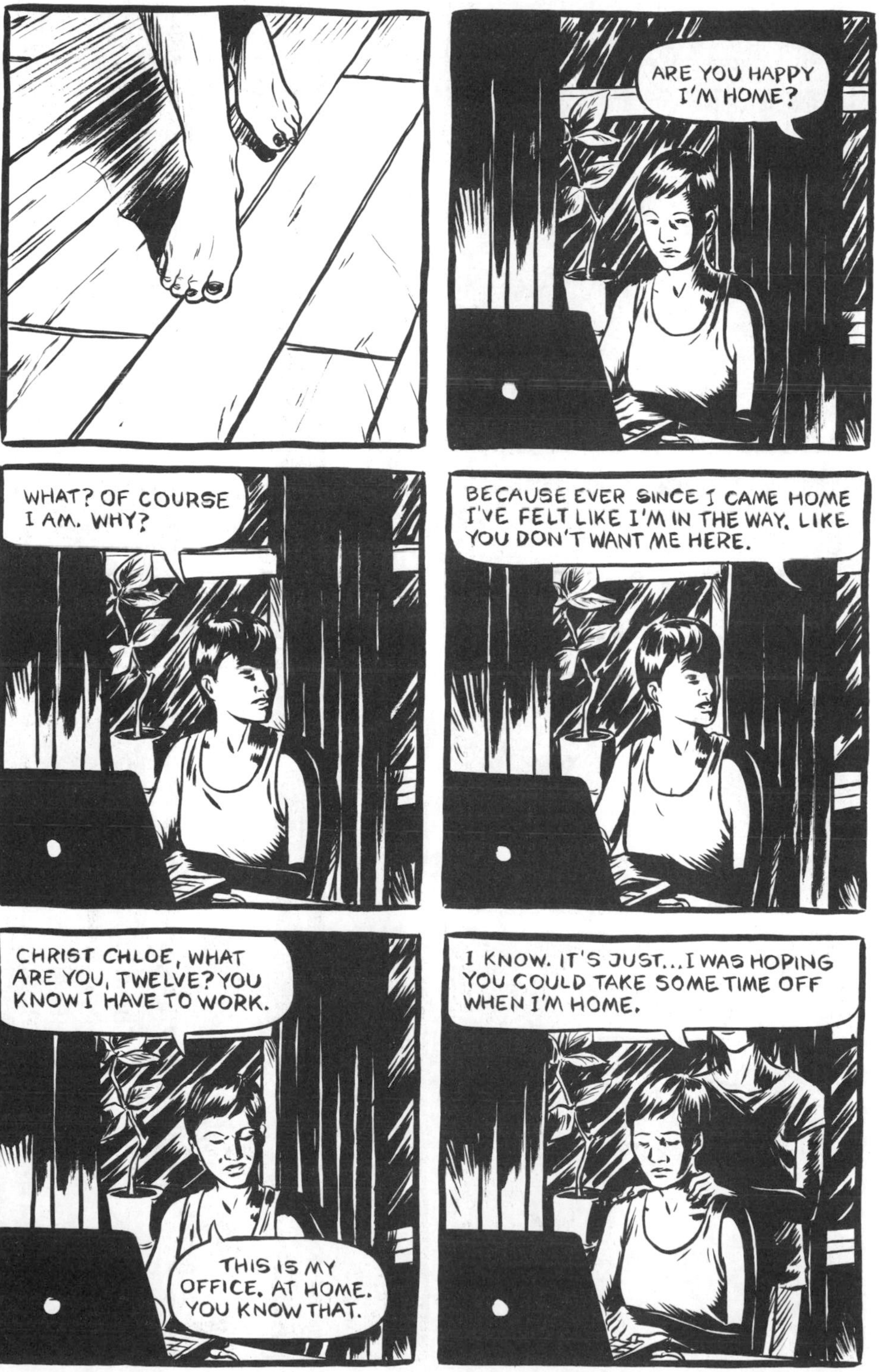
ARE YOU HAPPY I'M HOME?
WHAT? OF COURSE I AM. WHY?
BECAUSE EVER SINCE I CAME HOME I'VE FELT LIKE I'M IN THE WAY. LIKE YOU DON'T WANT ME HERE.
CHRIST CHLOE, WHAT ARE YOU, TWELVE? YOU KNOW I HAVE TO WORK.
THIS IS MY OFFICE. AT HOME. YOU KNOW THAT.
I KNOW. IT'S JUST...I WAS HOPING YOU COULD TAKE SOME TIME OFF WHEN I'M HOME.

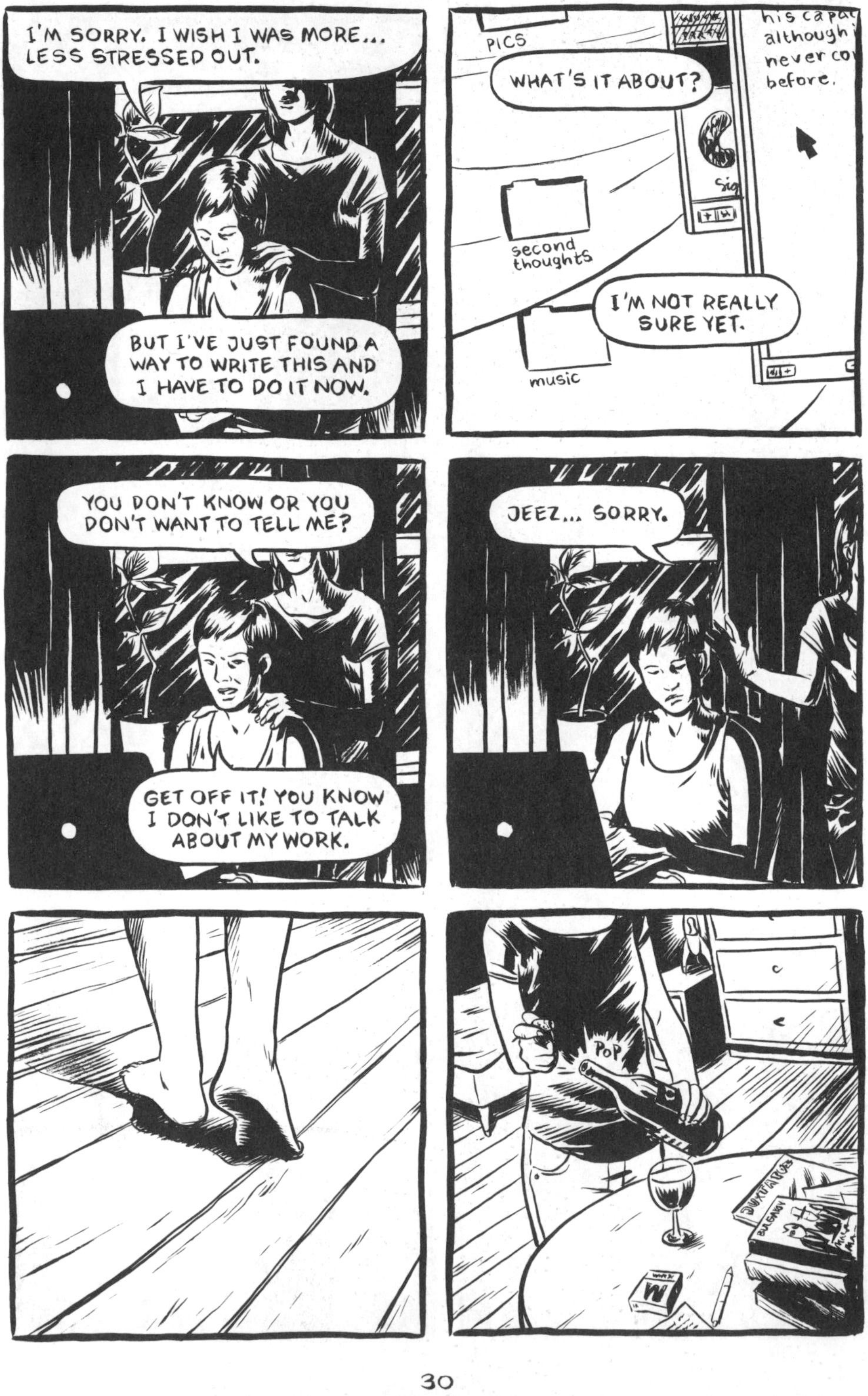
I'M SORRY. I WISH I WAS MORE... LESS STRESSED OUT.
BUT I'VE JUST FOUND A WAY TO WRITE THIS AND I HAVE TO DO IT NOW.
PICS
WHAT'S IT ABOUT?
although
before.
second thoughts
I'M NOT REALLY SURE YET.
music
YOU DON'T KNOW OR YOU DON'T WANT TO TELL ME?
GET OFF IT! YOU KNOW I DON'T LIKE TO TALK ABOUT MY WORK.
JEEZ... SORRY.
POP

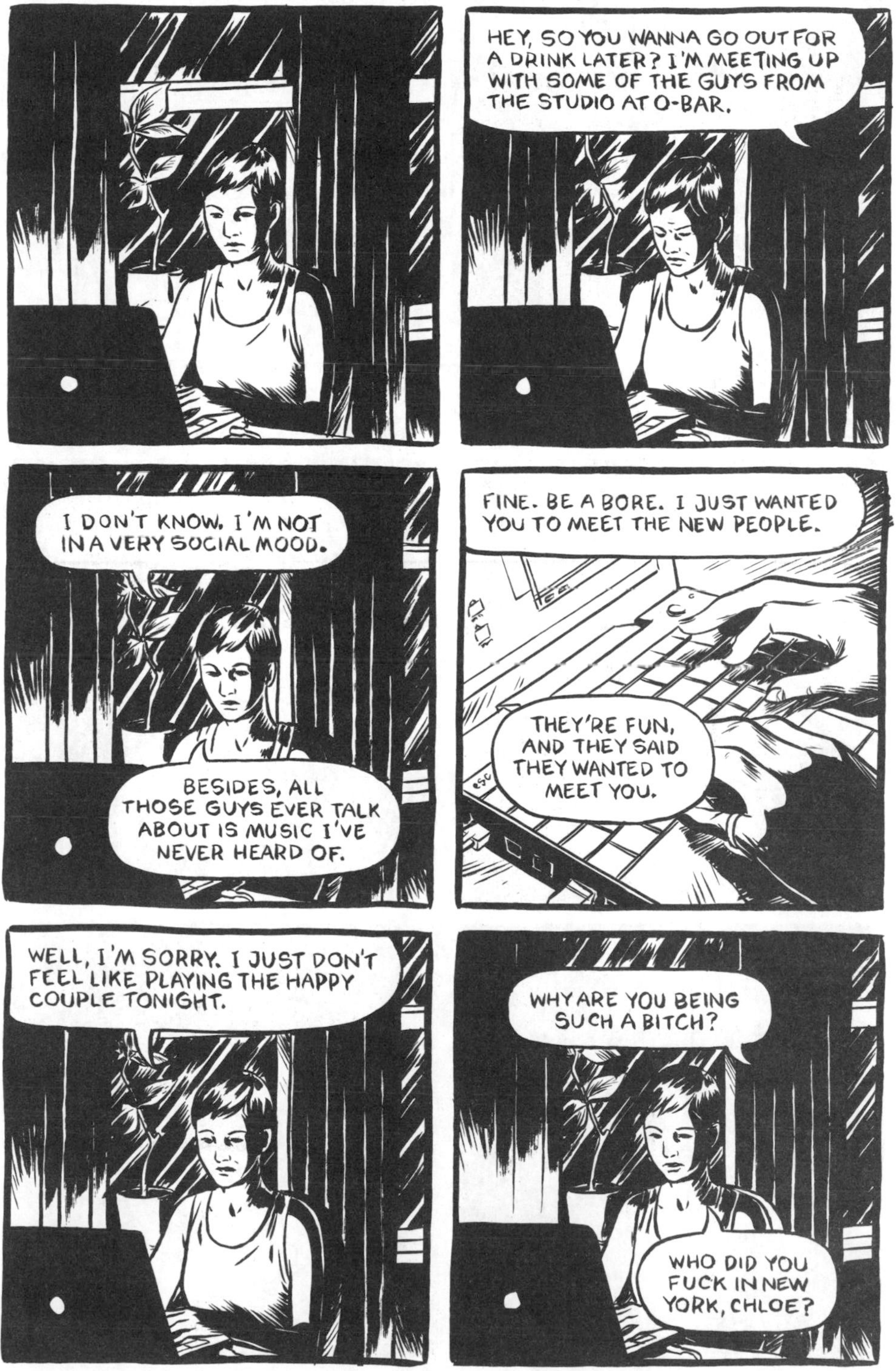
HEY, SO YOU WANNA GO OUT FOR A DRINK LATER? I'M MEETING UP WITH SOME OF THE GUYS FROM THE STUDIO AT O-BAR.
I DON'T KNOW. I'M NOT IN A VERY SOCIAL MOOD.
BESIDES, ALL THOSE GUYS EVER TALK ABOUT IS MUSIC I'VE NEVER HEARD OF.
FINE. BE A BORE. I JUST WANTED YOU TO MEET THE NEW PEOPLE.
THEY'RE FUN, AND THEY SAID THEY WANTED TO MEET YOU.
ESC
WELL, I'M SORRY. I JUST DON'T FEEL LIKE PLAYING THE HAPPY COUPLE TONIGHT.
WHY ARE YOU BEING SUCH A BITCH?
WHO DID YOU FUCK IN NEW YORK, CHLOE?

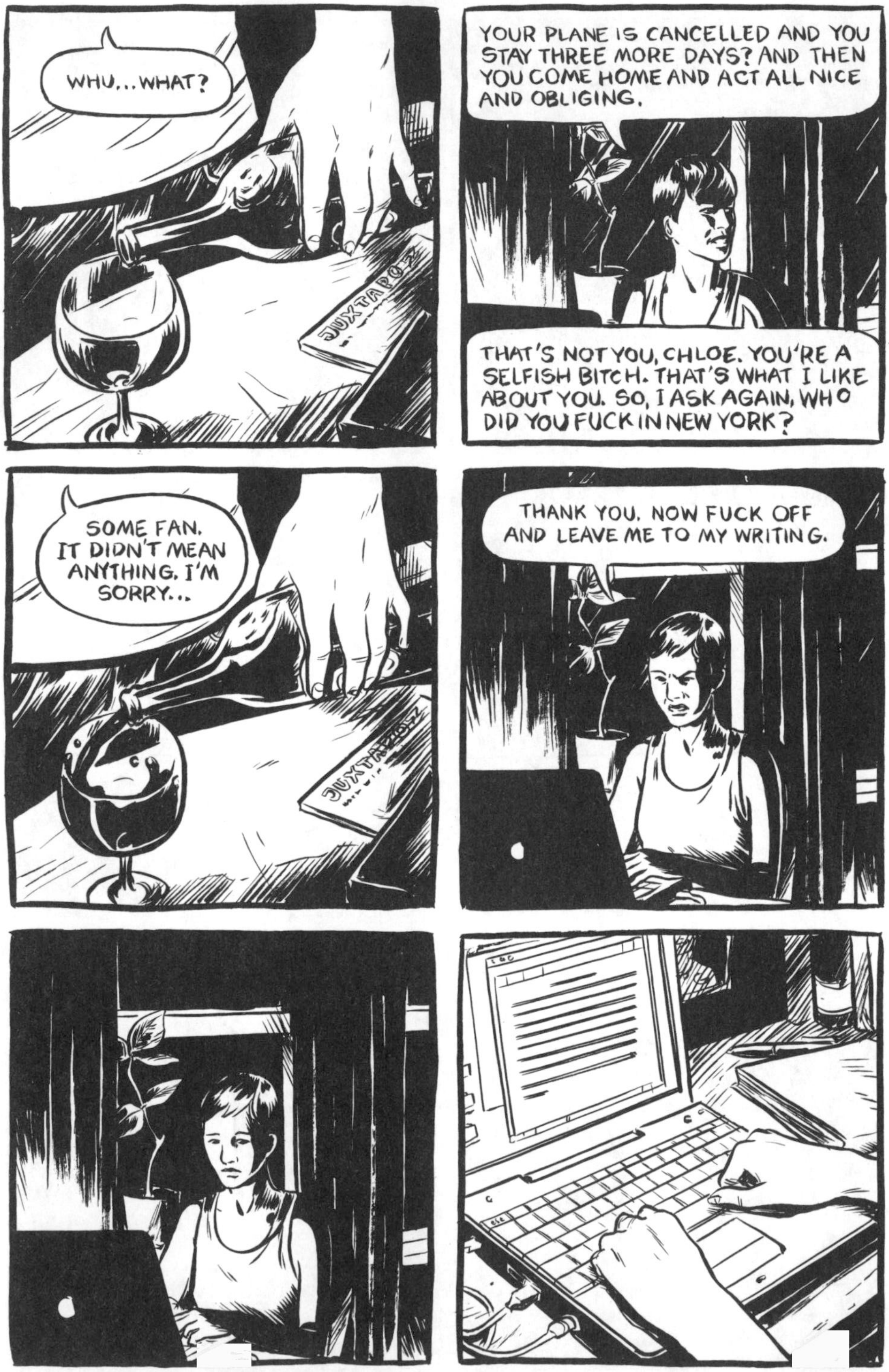
WHU... WHAT?
YOUR PLANE IS CANCELLED AND YOU STAY THREE MORE DAYS? AND THEN YOU COME HOME AND ACT ALL NICE AND OBLIGING.
THAT'S NOT YOU, CHLOE. YOU'RE A SELFISH BITCH. THAT'S WHAT I LIKE ABOUT YOU. SO, I ASK AGAIN, WHO DID YOU FUCK IN NEW YORK?
JUXTAPOZ
SOME FAN. IT DIDN'T MEAN ANYTHING. I'M SORRY...
THANK YOU. NOW FUCK OFF AND LEAVE ME TO MY WRITING.

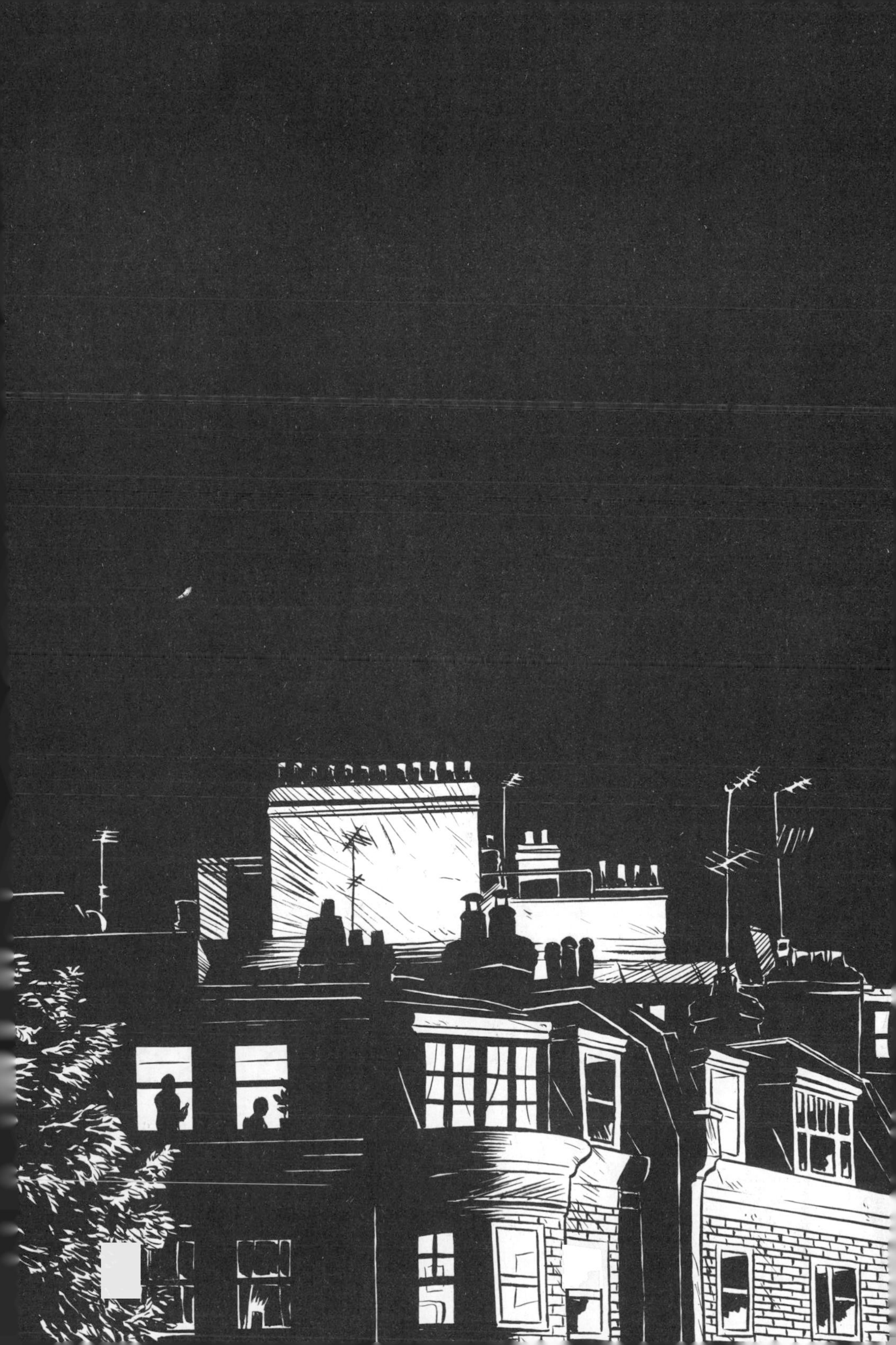

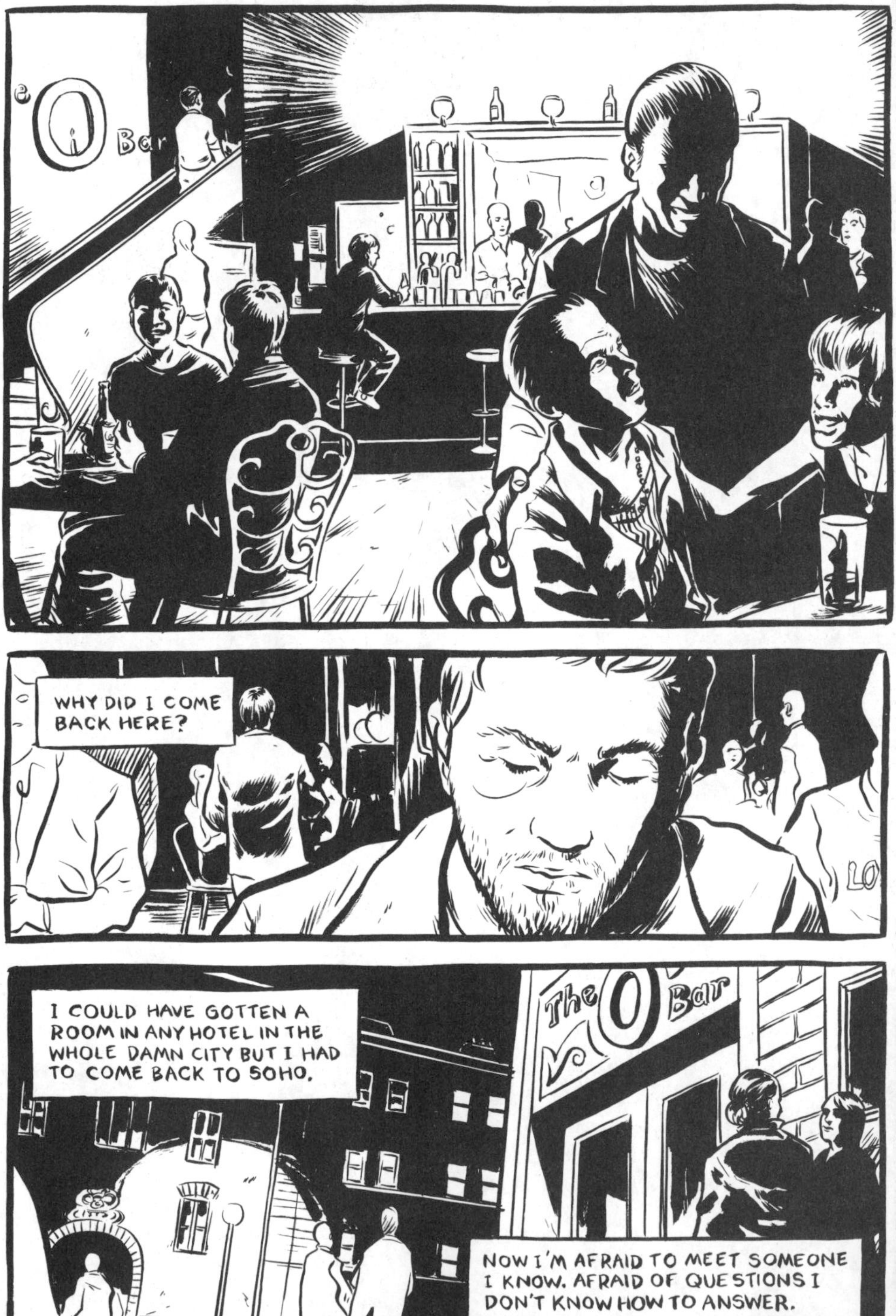
The O Bar
WHY DID I COME BACK HERE?
I COULD HAVE GOTTEN A ROOM IN ANY HOTEL IN THE WHOLE DAMN CITY BUT I HAD TO COME BACK TO SOHO.
The O Bar
NOW I'M AFRAID TO MEET SOMEONE I KNOW. AFRAID OF QUESTIONS I DON'T KNOW HOW TO ANSWER.

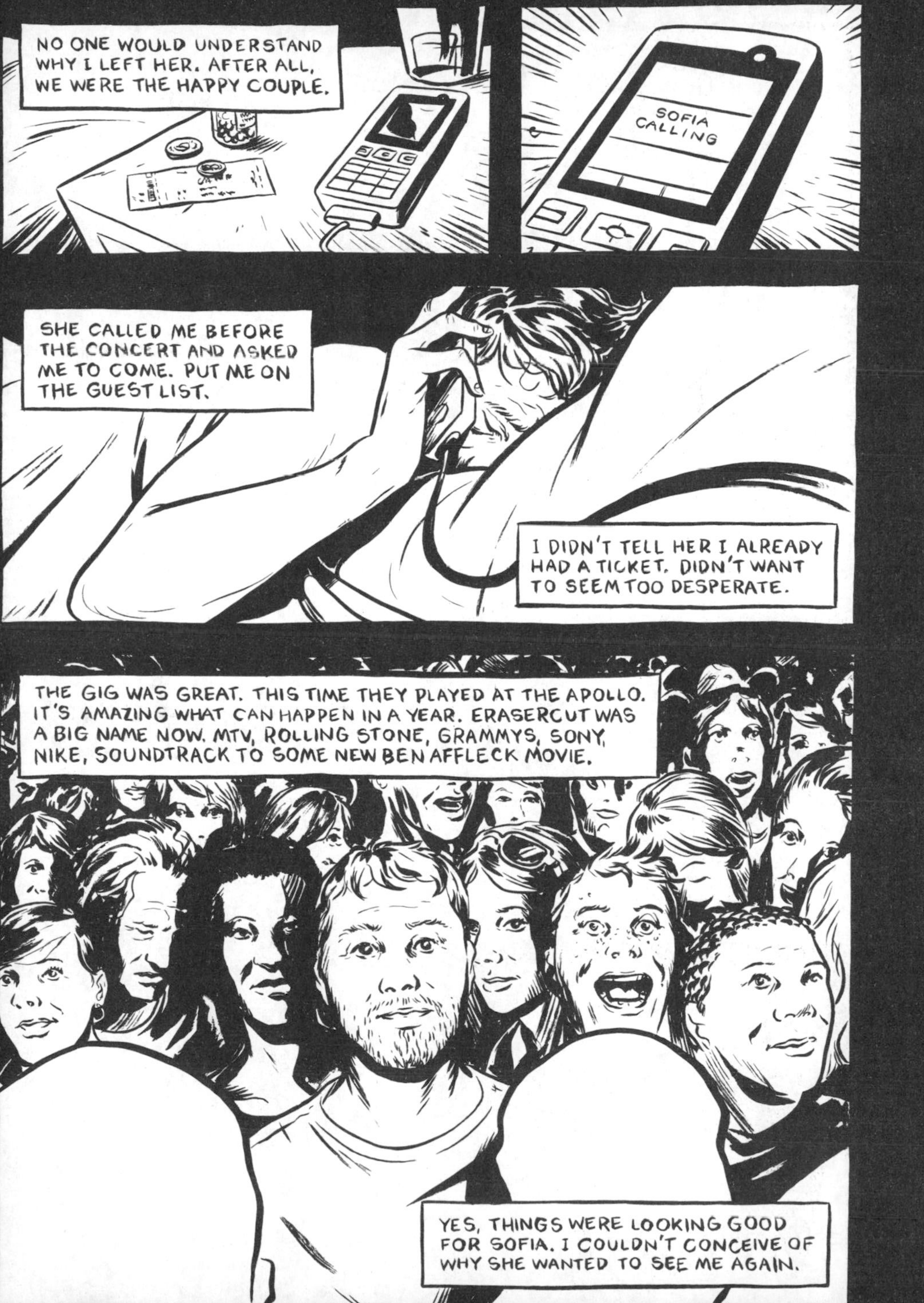
NO ONE WOULD UNDERSTAND WHY I LEFT HER. AFTER ALL, WE WERE THE HAPPY COUPLE.
SOFIA CALLING
SHE CALLED ME BEFORE THE CONCERT AND ASKED ME TO COME. PUT ME ON THE GUEST LIST.
I DIDN'T TELL HER I ALREADY HAD A TICKET. DIDN'T WANT TO SEEM TOO DESPERATE.
THE GIG WAS GREAT. THIS TIME THEY PLAYED AT THE APOLLO. IT'S AMAZING WHAT CAN HAPPEN IN A YEAR. ERASERCUT WAS A BIG NAME NOW. MTV, ROLLING STONE, GRAMMYS, SONY, NIKE, SOUNDTRACK TO SOME NEW BEN AFFLECK MOVIE.
YES, THINGS WERE LOOKING GOOD FOR SOFIA. I COULDN'T CONCEIVE OF WHY SHE WANTED TO SEE ME AGAIN.

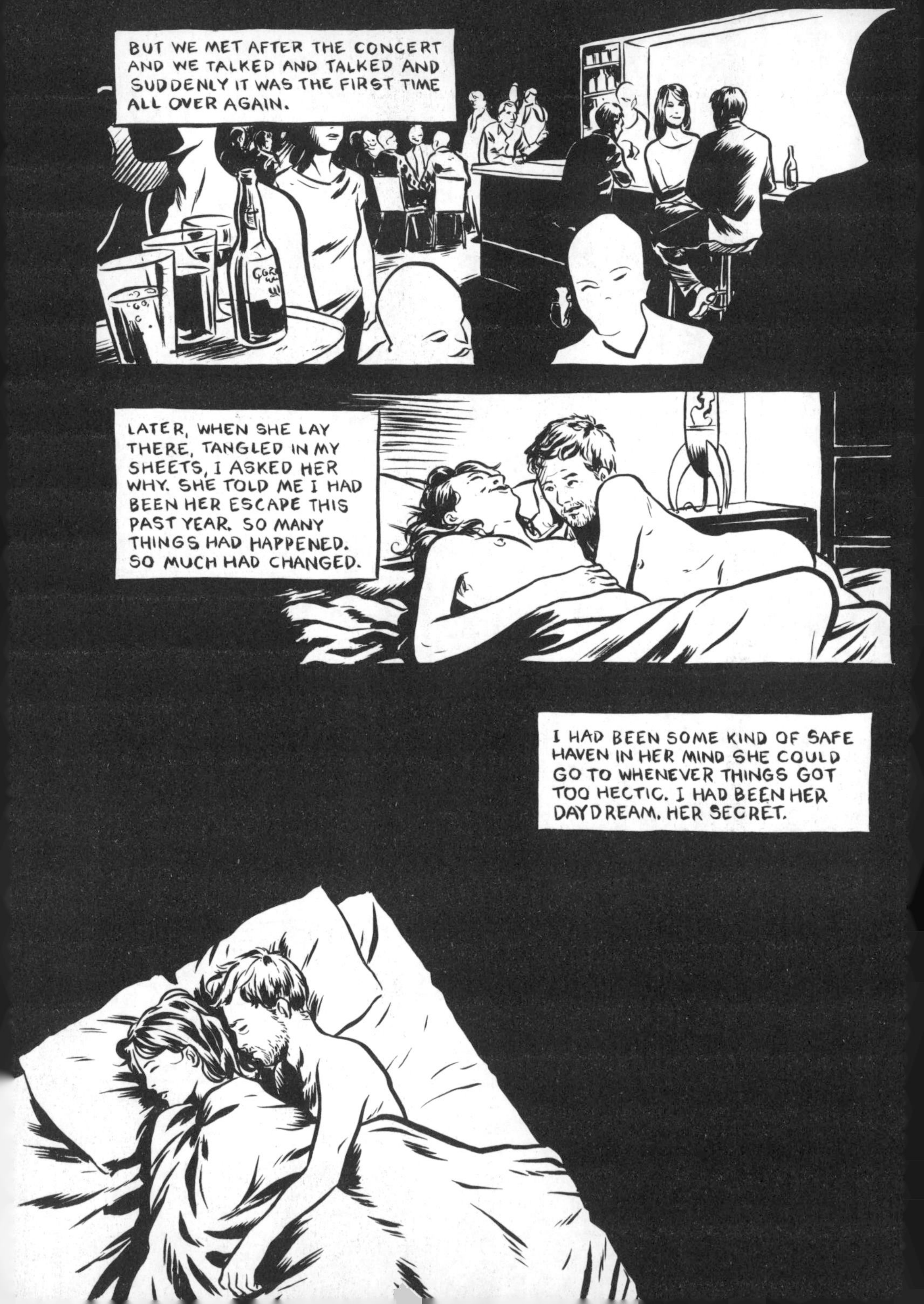
BUT WE MET AFTER THE CONCERT AND WE TALKED AND TALKED AND SUDDENLY IT WAS THE FIRST TIME ALL OVER AGAIN.
LATER, WHEN SHE LAY THERE, TANGLED IN MY SHEETS, I ASKED HER WHY. SHE TOLD ME I HAD BEEN HER ESCAPE THIS PAST YEAR. SO MANY THINGS HAD HAPPENED. SO MUCH HAD CHANGED.
I HAD BEEN SOME KIND OF SAFE HAVEN IN HER MIND SHE COULD GO TO WHENEVER THINGS GOT TOO HECTIC. I HAD BEEN HER DAYDREAM. HER SECRET.

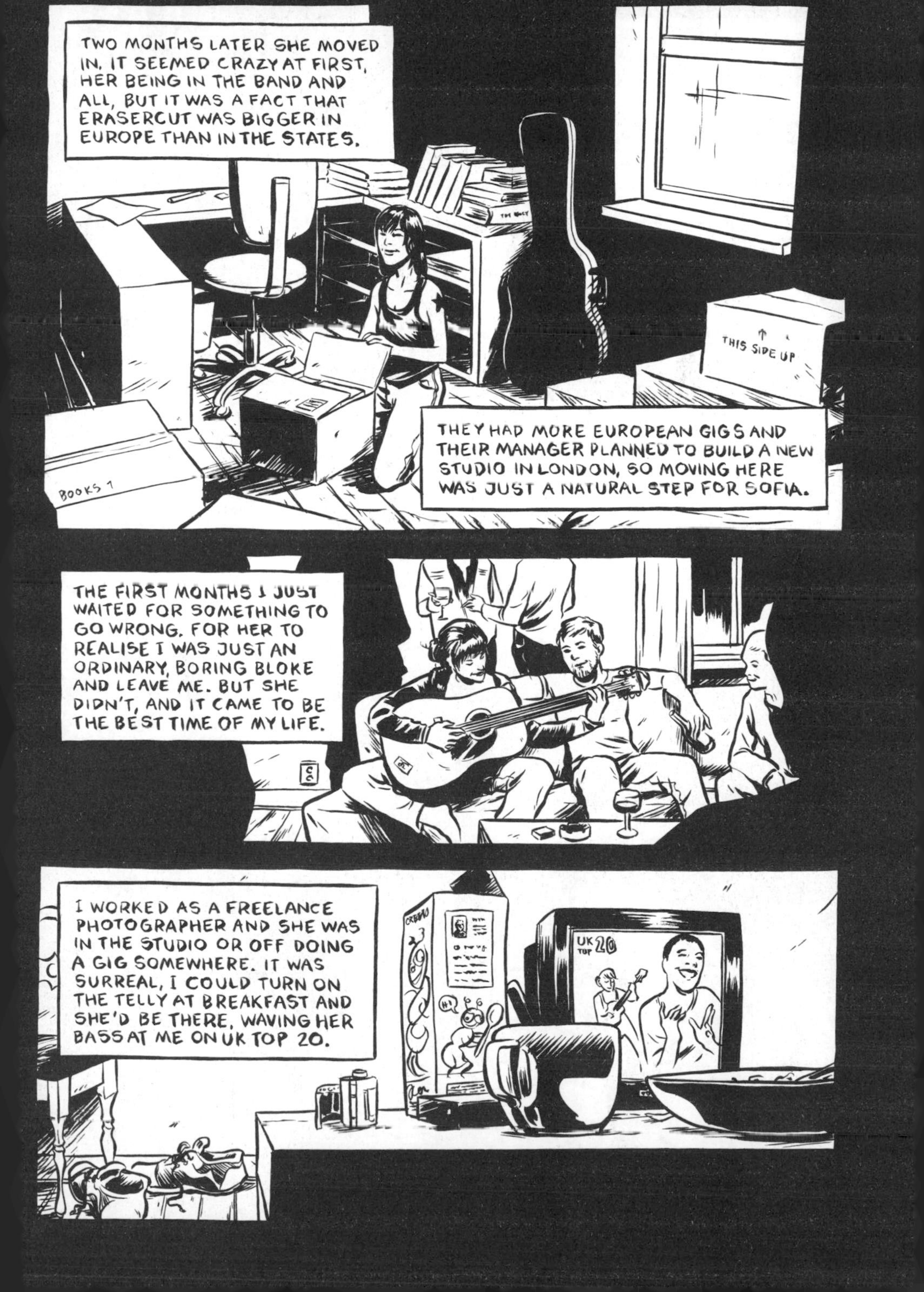
TWO MONTHS LATER SHE MOVED IN. IT SEEMED CRAZY AT FIRST, HER BEING IN THE BAND AND ALL, BUT IT WAS A FACT THAT ERASERCUT WAS BIGGER IN EUROPE THAN IN THE STATES.
THIS SIDE UP
BOOKS 1
THEY HAD MORE EUROPEAN GIGS AND THEIR MANAGER PLANNED TO BUILD A NEW STUDIO IN LONDON, SO MOVING HERE WAS JUST A NATURAL STEP FOR SOFIA.
THE FIRST MONTHS I JUST WAITED FOR SOMETHING TO GO WRONG. FOR HER TO REALISE I WAS JUST AN ORDINARY, BORING BLOKE AND LEAVE ME. BUT SHE DIDN'T, AND IT CAME TO BE THE BEST TIME OF MY LIFE.
I WORKED AS A FREELANCE PHOTOGRAPHER AND SHE WAS IN THE STUDIO OR OFF DOING A GIG SOMEWHERE. IT WAS SURREAL, I COULD TURN ON THE TELLY AT BREAKFAST AND SHE'D BE THERE, WAVING HER BASS AT ME ON UK TOP 20.
UK TOP 20

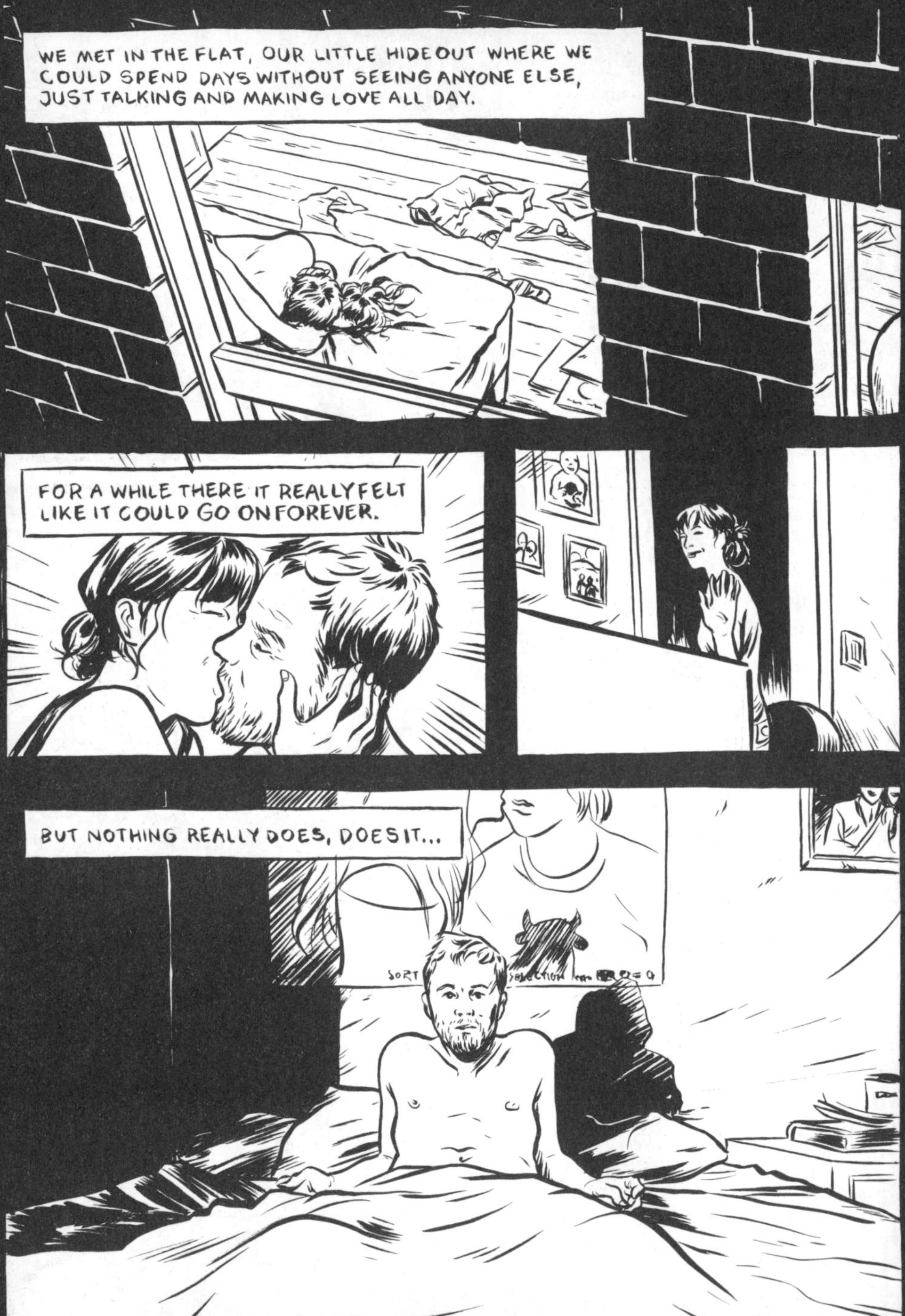
WE MET IN THE FLAT, OUR LITTLE HIDEOUT WHERE WE COULD SPEND DAYS WITHOUT SEEING ANYONE ELSE, JUST TALKING AND MAKING LOVE ALL DAY.
FOR A WHILE THERE IT REALLY FELT LIKE IT COULD GO ON FOREVER.
BUT NOTHING REALLY DOES, DOES IT...

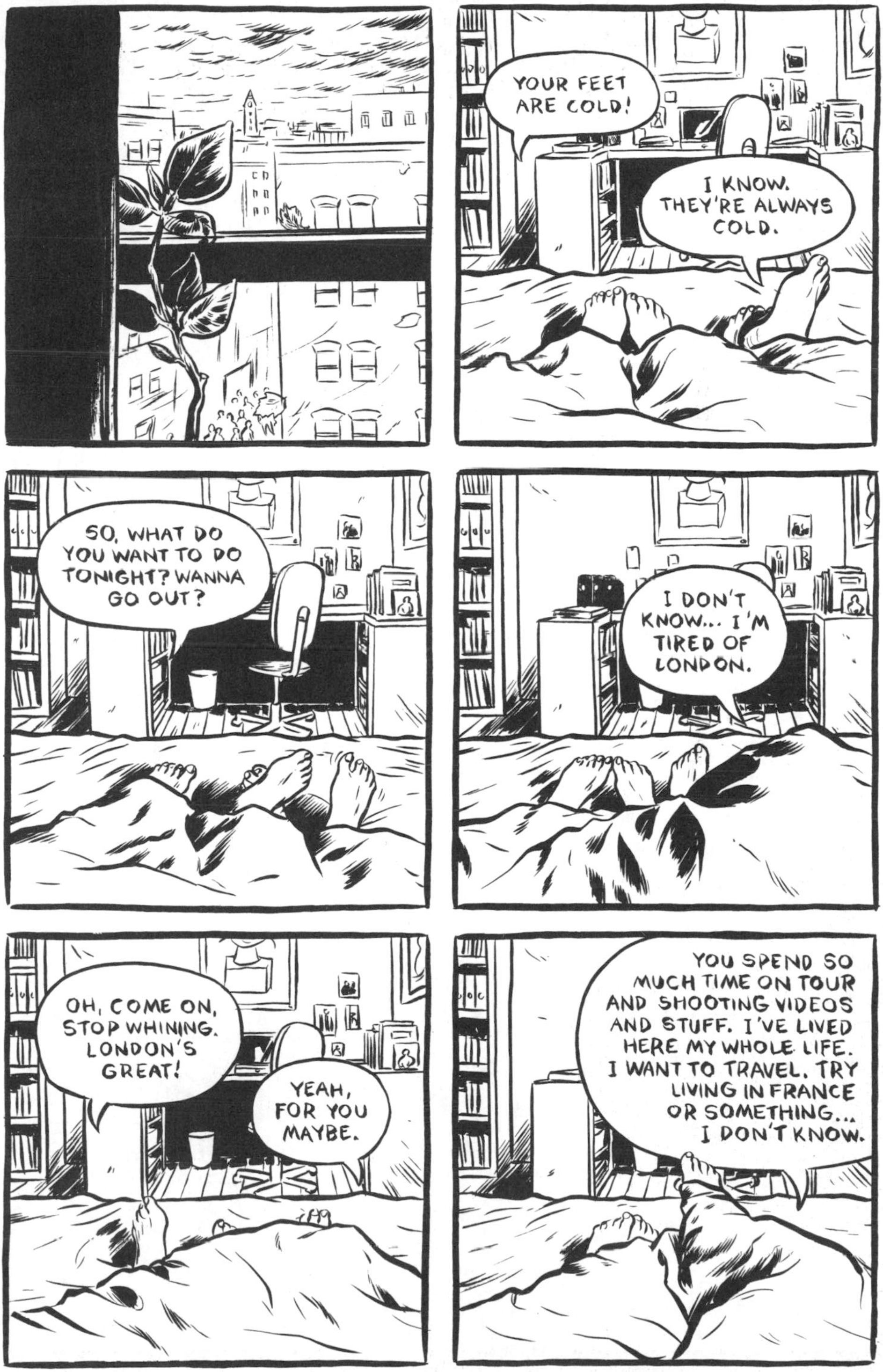

YOUR FEET ARE COLD!
I KNOW. THEY'RE ALWAYS COLD.
SO, WHAT DO YOU WANT TO DO TONIGHT? WANNA GO OUT?
I DON'T KNOW... I'M TIRED OF LONDON.
OH, COME ON, STOP WHINING. LONDON'S GREAT!
YEAH, FOR YOU MAYBE.
YOU SPEND SO MUCH TIME ON TOUR AND SHOOTING VIDEOS AND STUFF. I'VE LIVED HERE MY WHOLE LIFE. I WANT TO TRAVEL. TRY LIVING IN FRANCE OR SOMETHING... I DON'T KNOW.

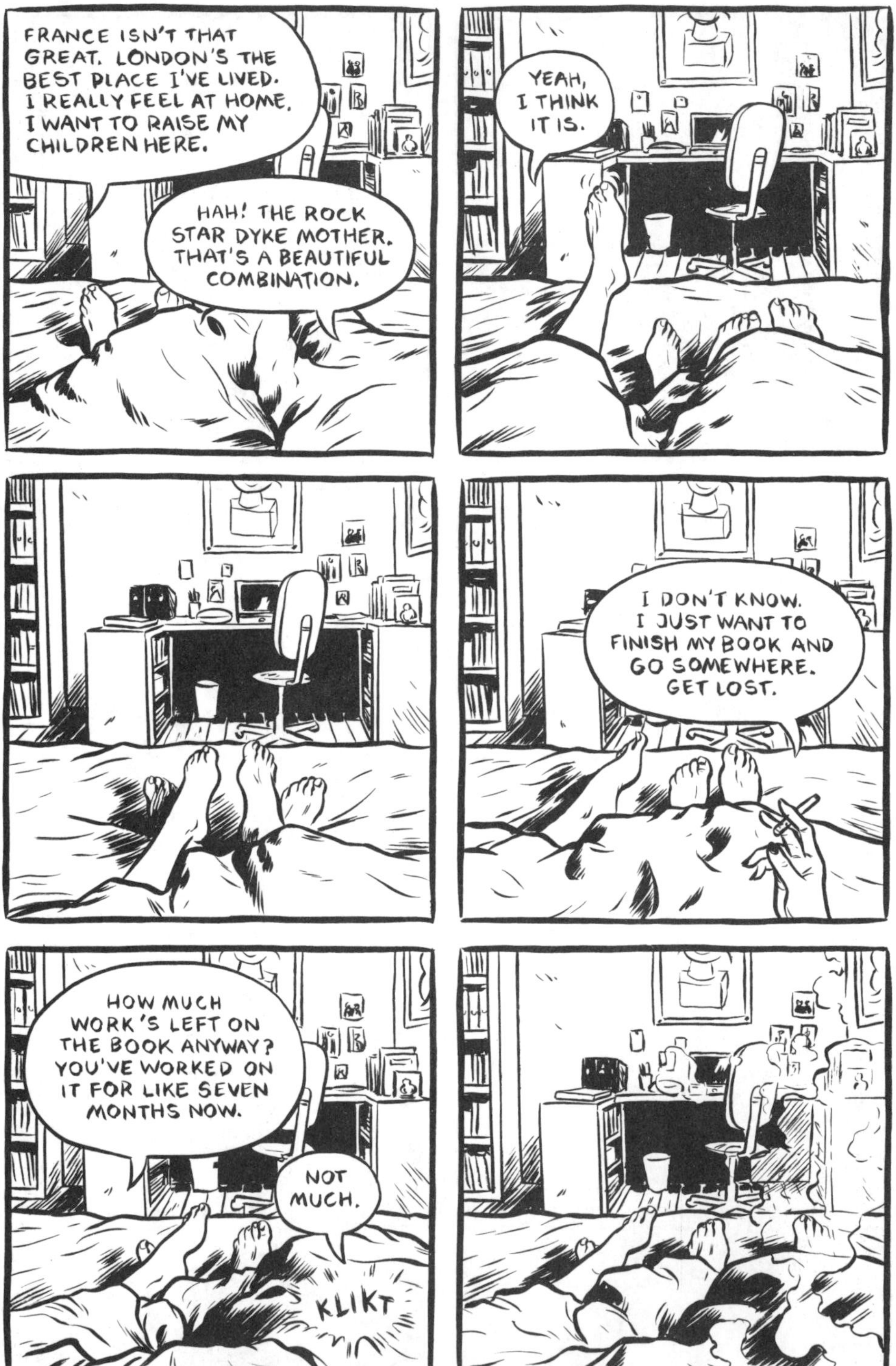
FRANCE ISN'T THAT GREAT. LONDON'S THE BEST PLACE I'VE LIVED. I REALLY FEEL AT HOME. I WANT TO RAISE MY CHILDREN HERE.
HAH! THE ROCK STAR DYKE MOTHER. THAT'S A BEAUTIFUL COMBINATION.
YEAH, I THINK IT IS.
I DON'T KNOW. I JUST WANT TO FINISH MY BOOK AND GO SOMEWHERE. GET LOST.
HOW MUCH WORK'S LEFT ON THE BOOK ANYWAY? YOU'VE WORKED ON IT FOR LIKE SEVEN MONTHS NOW.
NOT MUCH.
KLIKT

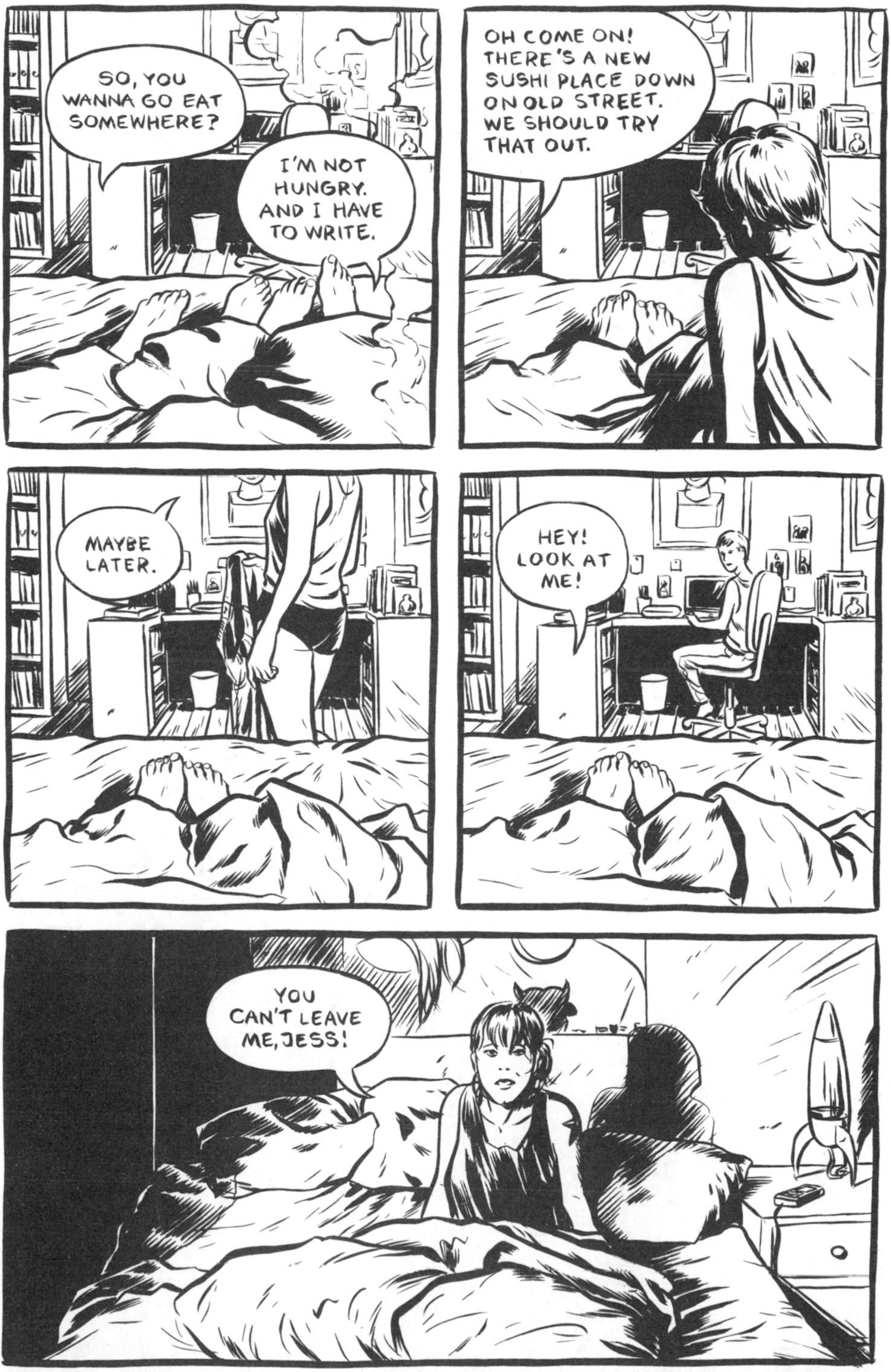
SO, YOU WANNA GO EAT SOMEWHERE?
I'M NOT HUNGRY. AND I HAVE TO WRITE.
OH COME ON! THERE'S A NEW SUSHI PLACE DOWN ON OLD STREET. WE SHOULD TRY THAT OUT.
MAYBE LATER.
HEY! LOOK AT ME!
YOU CAN'T LEAVE ME, JESS!

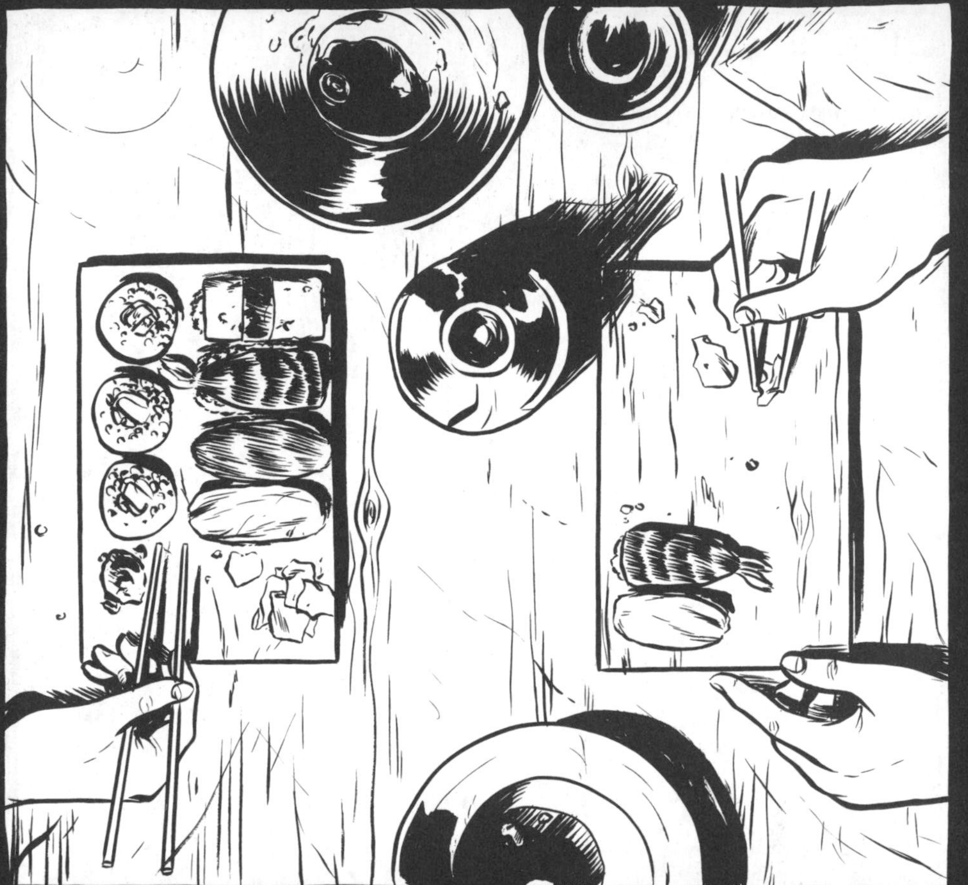

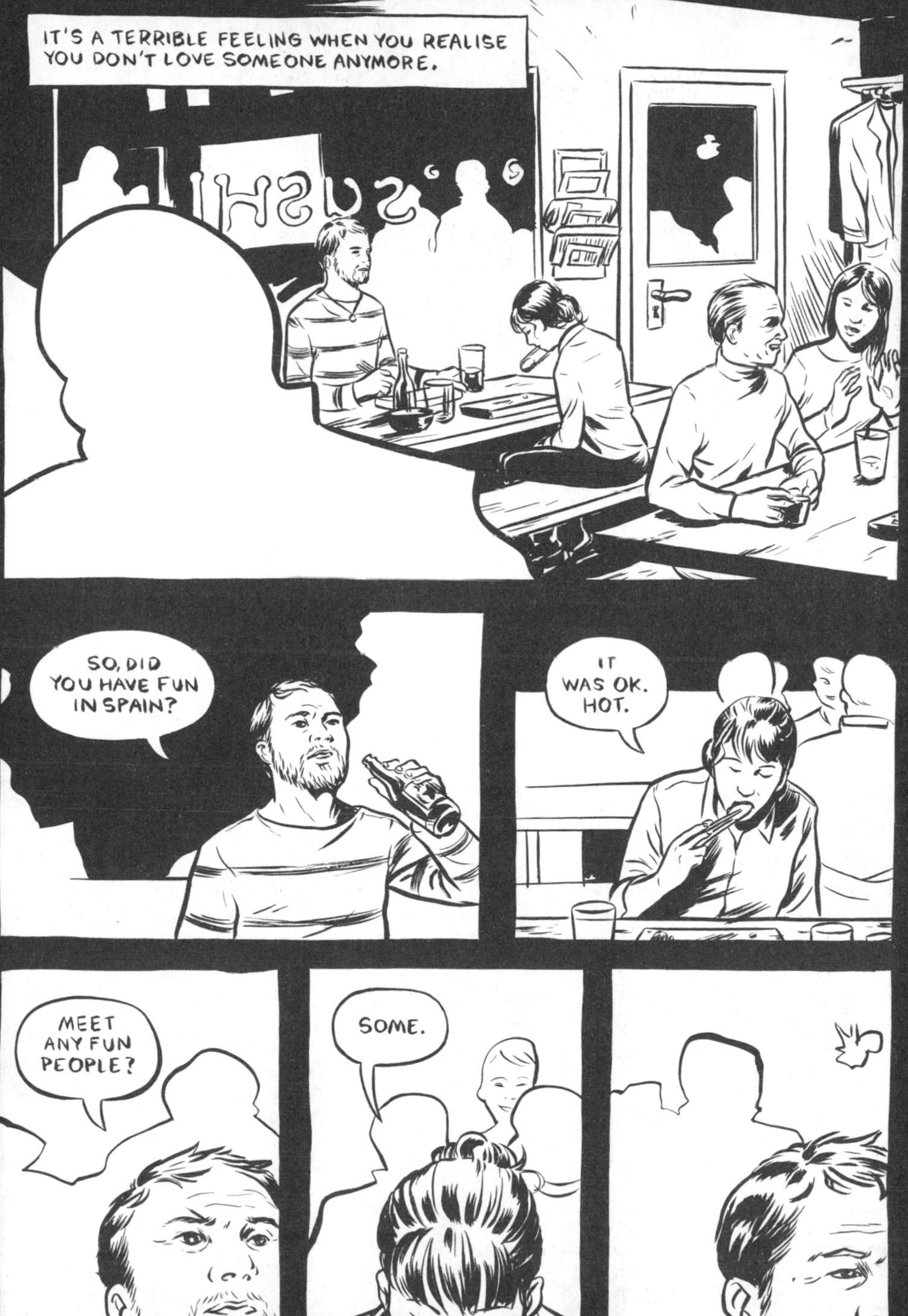
IT'S A TERRIBLE FEELING WHEN YOU REALISE YOU DON'T LOVE SOMEONE ANYMORE.
SUSHI
SO, DID YOU HAVE FUN IN SPAIN?
IT WAS OK. HOT.
MEET ANY FUN PEOPLE?
SOME.

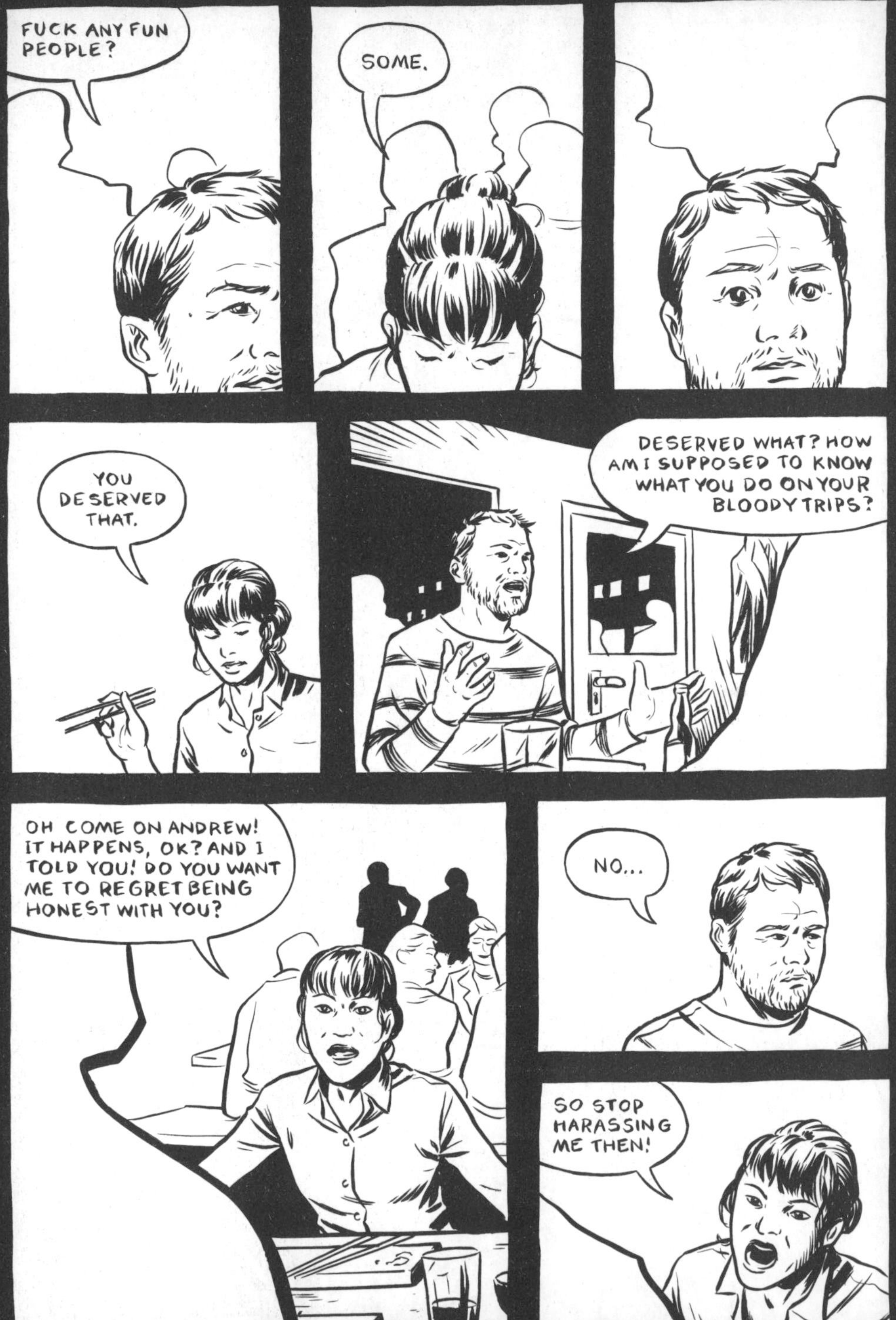
FUCK ANY FUN PEOPLE?
SOME.
YOU DESERVED THAT.
DESERVED WHAT? HOW AM I SUPPOSED TO KNOW WHAT YOU DO ON YOUR BLOODY TRIPS?
OH COME ON ANDREW! IT HAPPENS, OK? AND I TOLD YOU! DO YOU WANT ME TO REGRET BEING HONEST WITH YOU?
NO...
SO STOP HARASSING ME THEN!

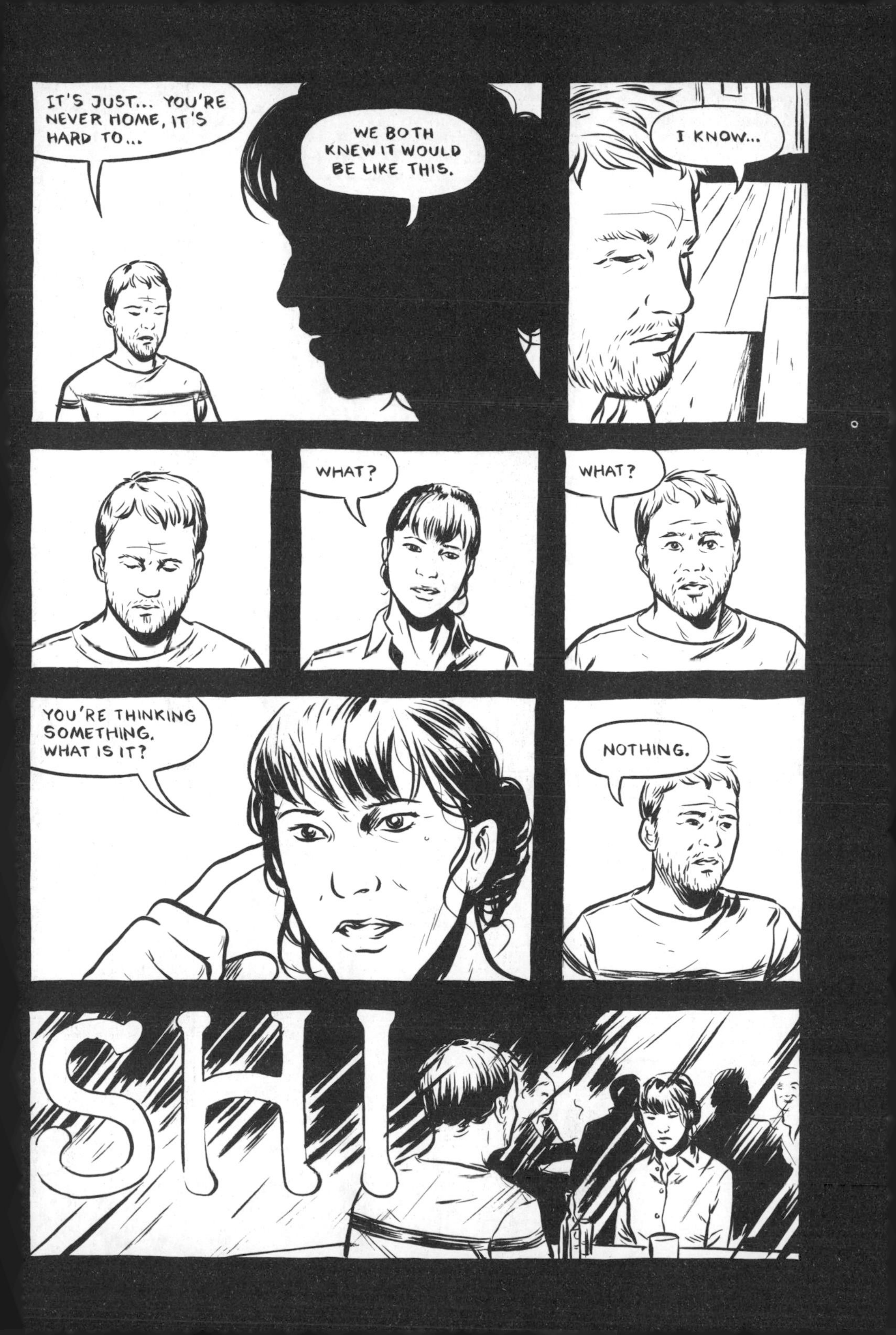
IT'S JUST... YOU'RE NEVER HOME, IT'S HARD TO...
WE BOTH KNEW IT WOULD BE LIKE THIS.
I KNOW...
WHAT?
WHAT?
YOU'RE THINKING SOMETHING. WHAT IS IT?
NOTHING.
SHI

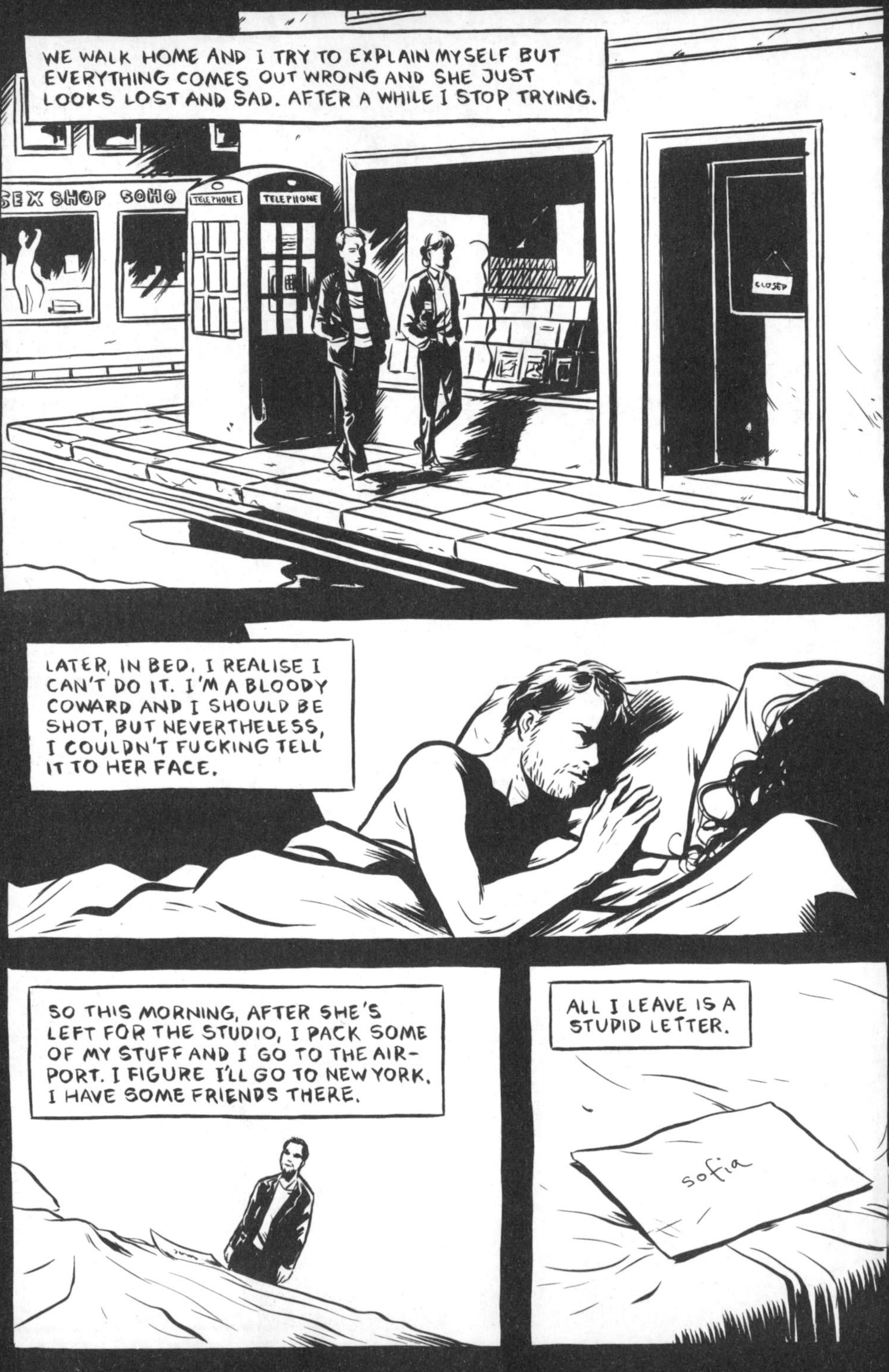
WE WALK HOME AND I TRY TO EXPLAIN MYSELF BUT EVERYTHING COMES OUT WRONG AND SHE JUST LOOKS LOST AND SAD. AFTER A WHILE I STOP TRYING.
SEX SHOP SOHO
TELEPHONE
TELEPHONE
CLOSED
LATER, IN BED, I REALISE I CAN'T DO IT. I'M A BLOODY COWARD AND I SHOULD BE SHOT, BUT NEVERTHELESS, I COULDN'T FUCKING TELL IT TO HER FACE.
SO THIS MORNING, AFTER SHE'S LEFT FOR THE STUDIO, I PACK SOME OF MY STUFF AND I GO TO THE AIR-PORT. I FIGURE I'LL GO TO NEW YORK. I HAVE SOME FRIENDS THERE.
ALL I LEAVE IS A STUPID LETTER.
sofia

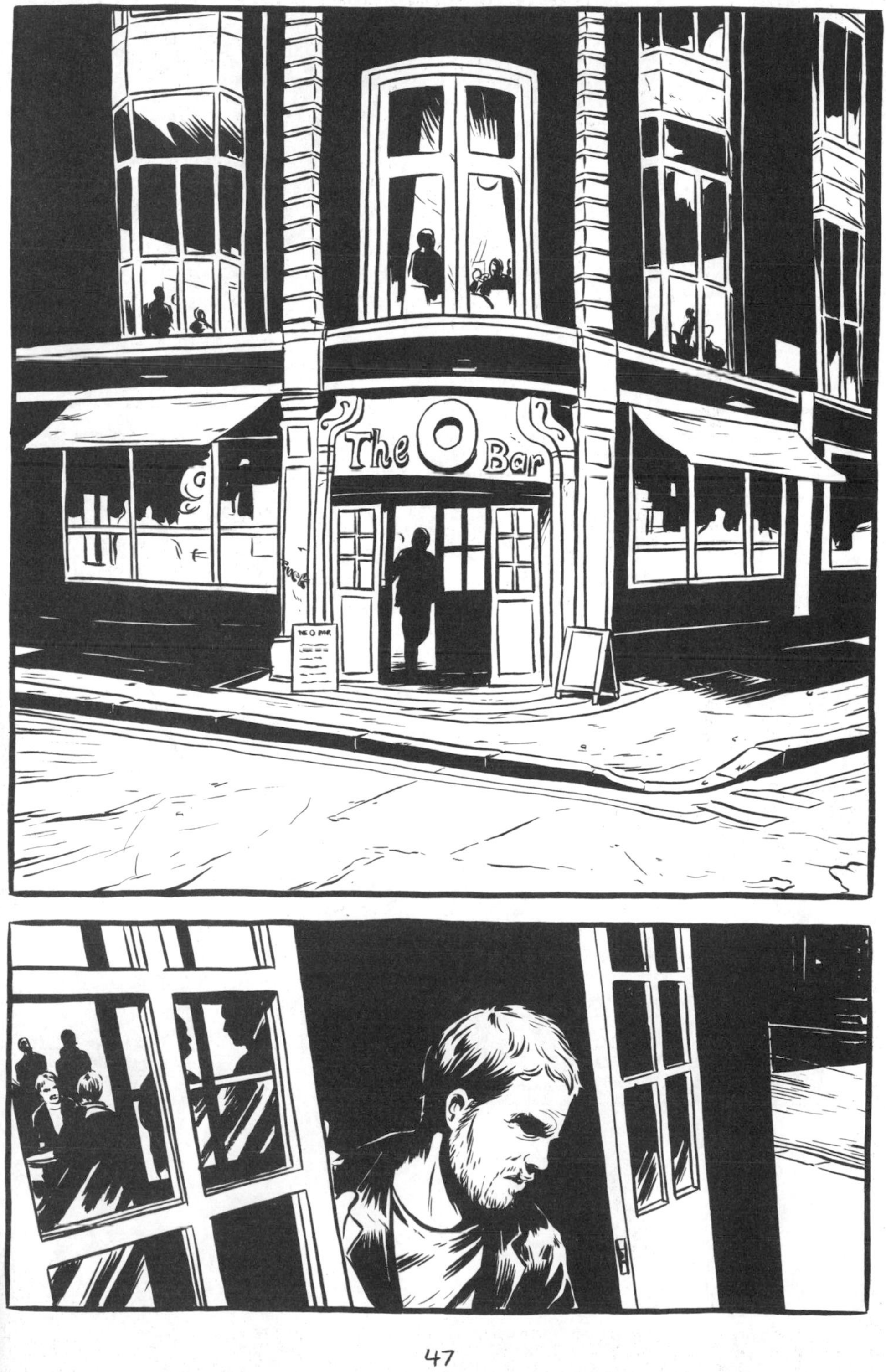
The O Bar
THE O BAR

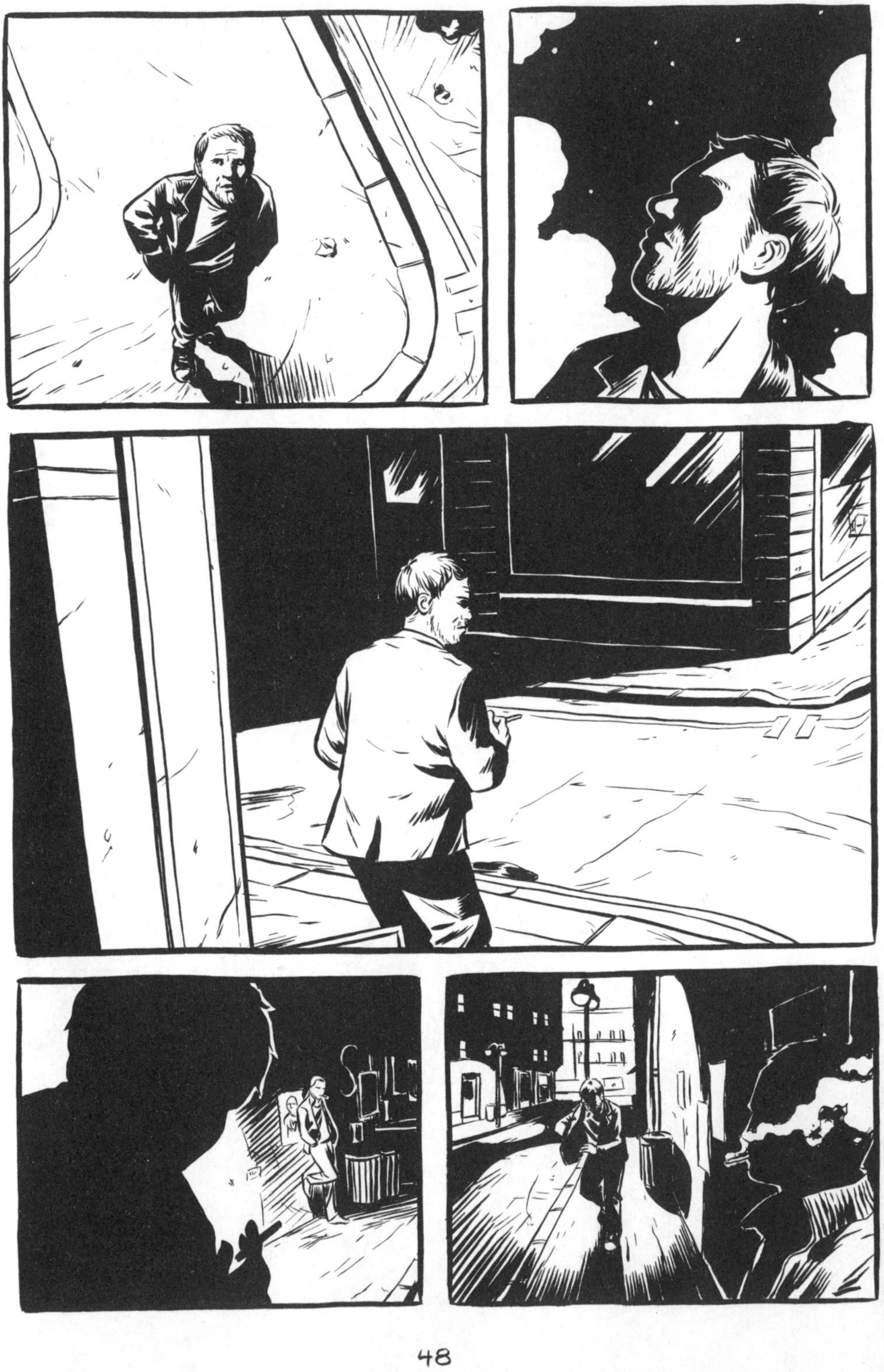

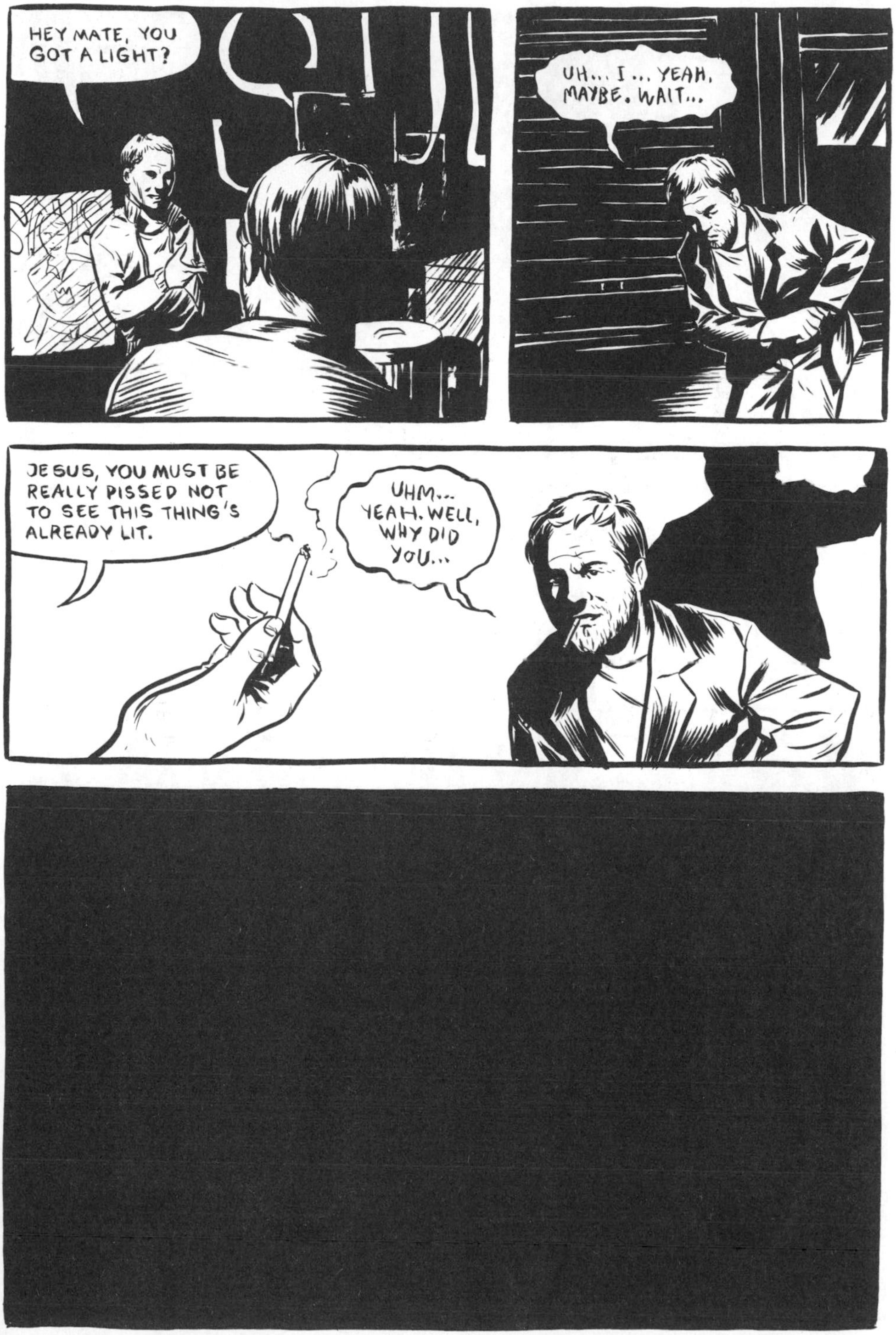
HEY MATE, YOU GOT A LIGHT?
UH... I... YEAH, MAYBE. WAIT...
JESUS, YOU MUST BE REALLY PISSED NOT TO SEE THIS THING'S ALREADY LIT.
UHM... YEAH. WELL, WHY DID YOU...

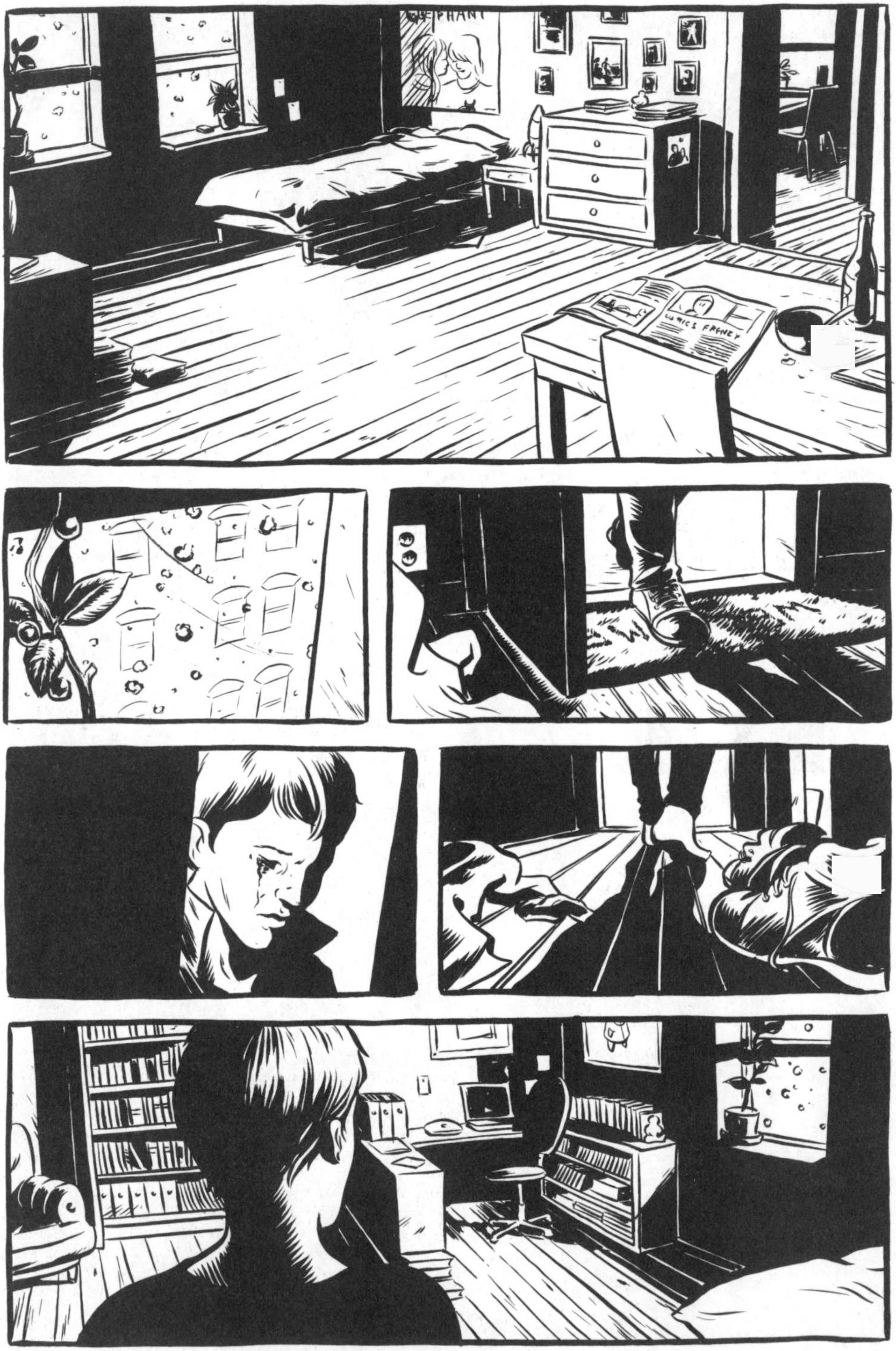
COMICS FRENZY

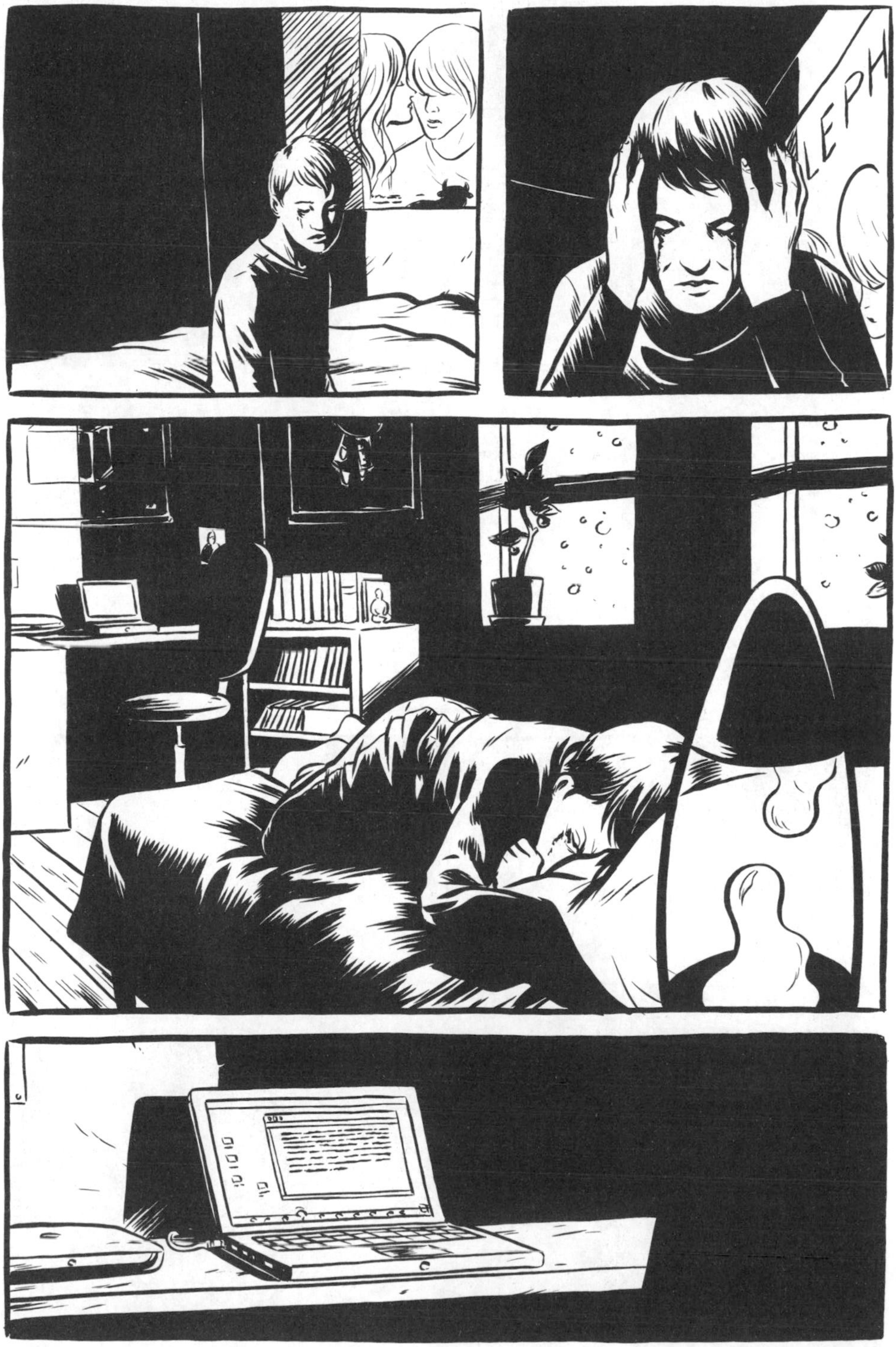
LEPH

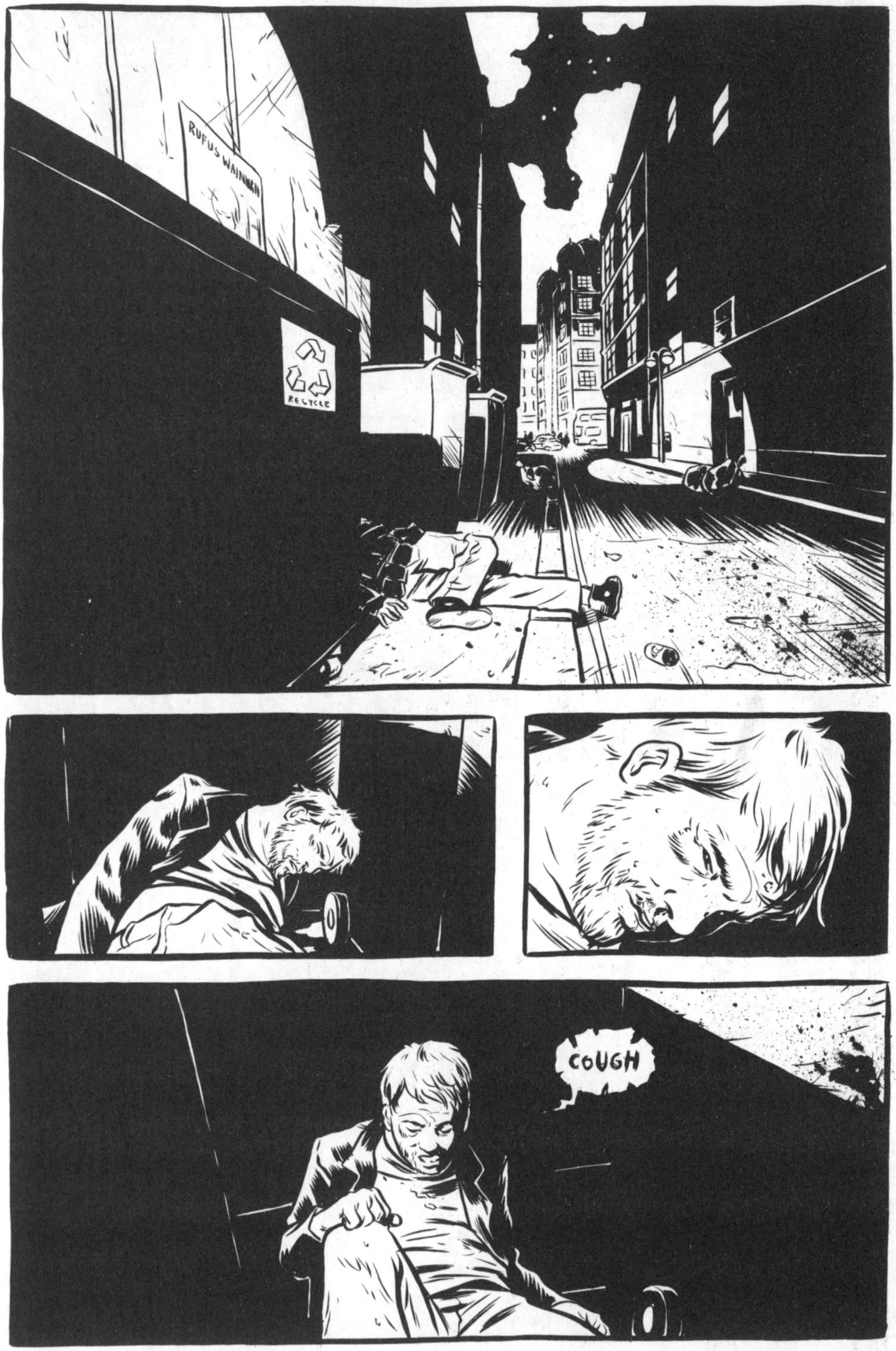
RUFUS WAIN
RECYCLE
COUGH

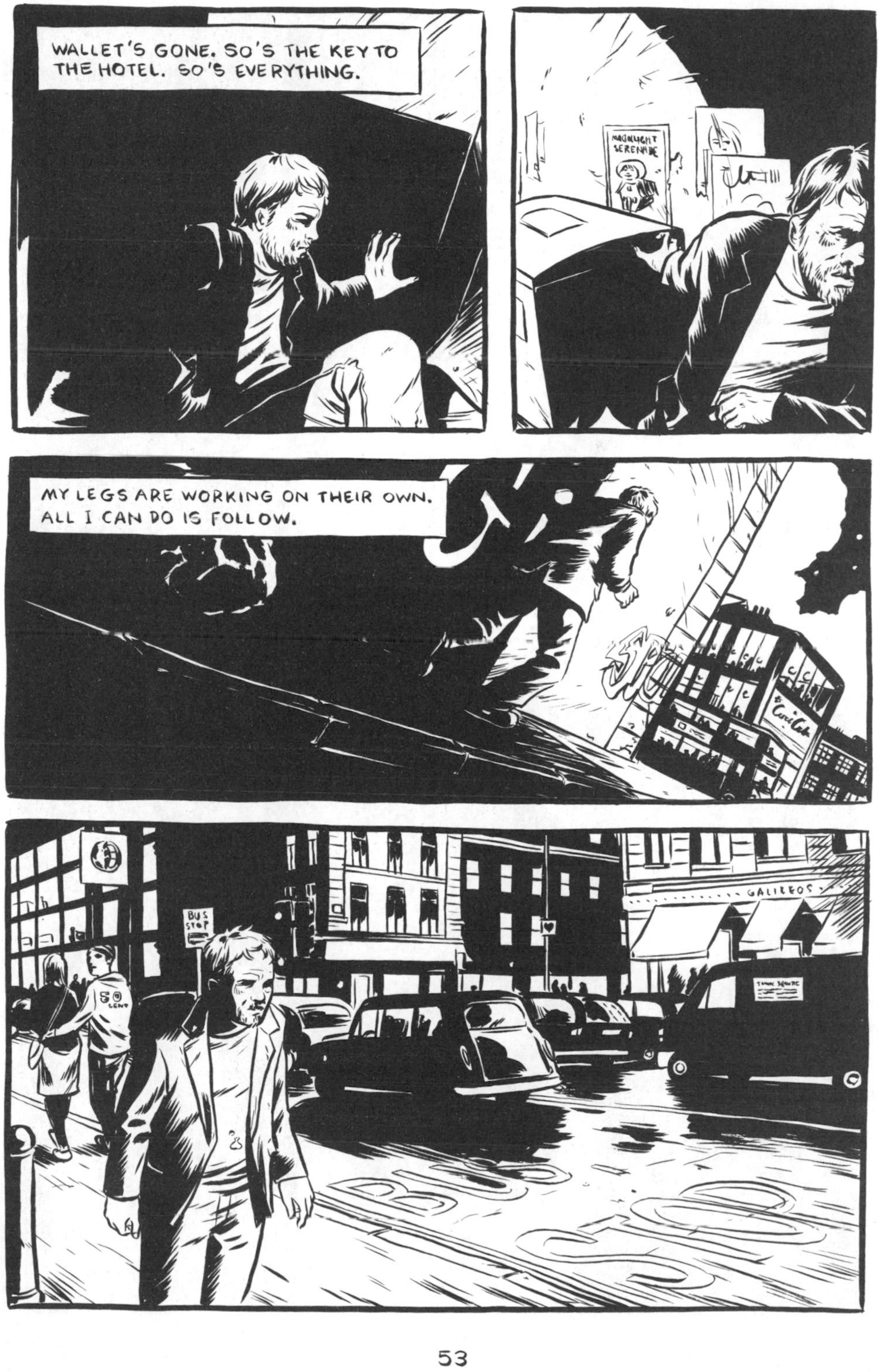
WALLET'S GONE. SO'S THE KEY TO THE HOTEL. SO'S EVERYTHING.
MY LEGS ARE WORKING ON THEIR OWN. ALL I CAN DO IS FOLLOW.
BUS STOP

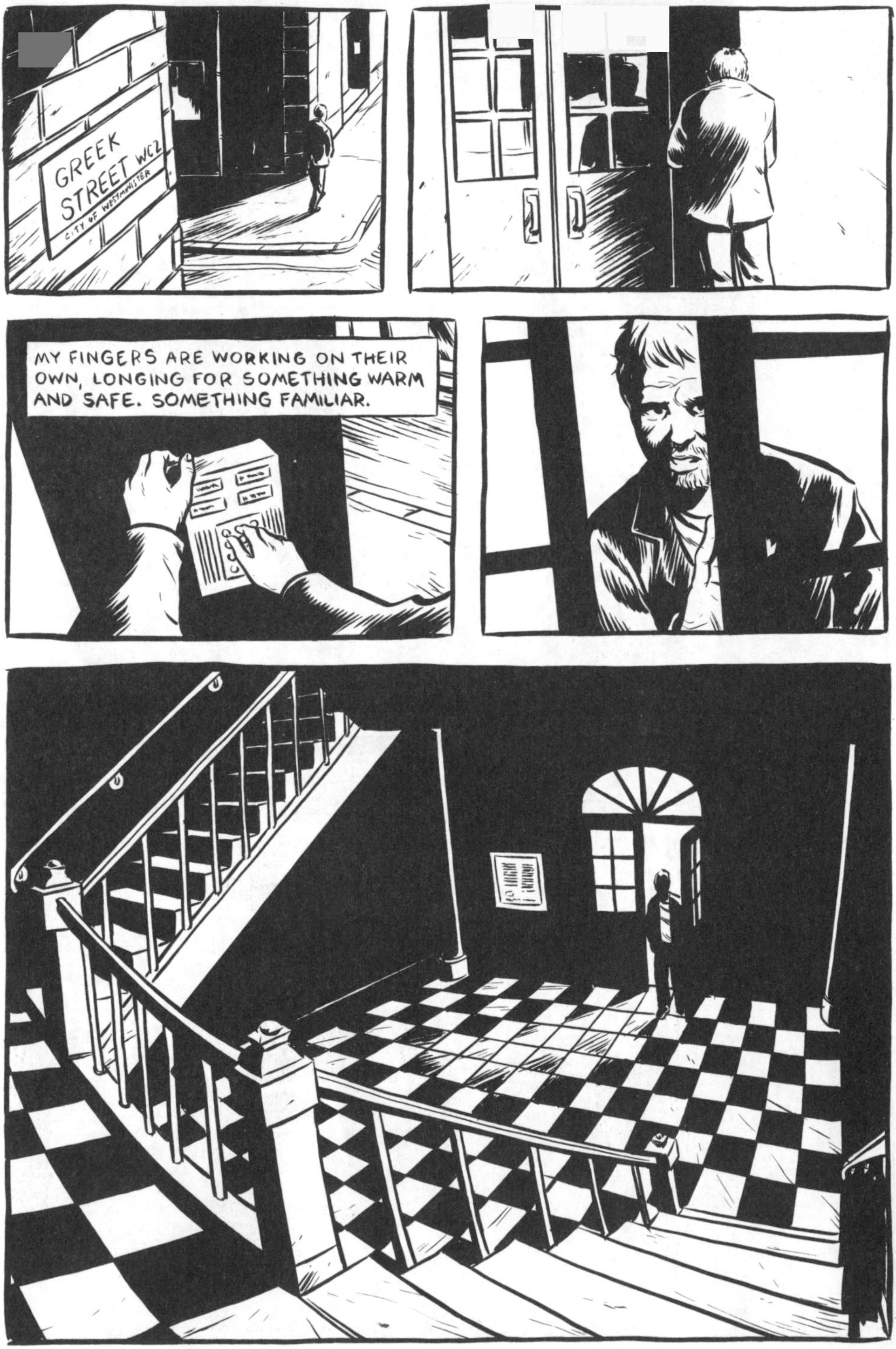
GREEK
STREET WC2
CITY OF WESTMINSTER
MY FINGERS ARE WORKING ON THEIR OWN, LONGING FOR SOMETHING WARM AND SAFE. SOMETHING FAMILIAR.

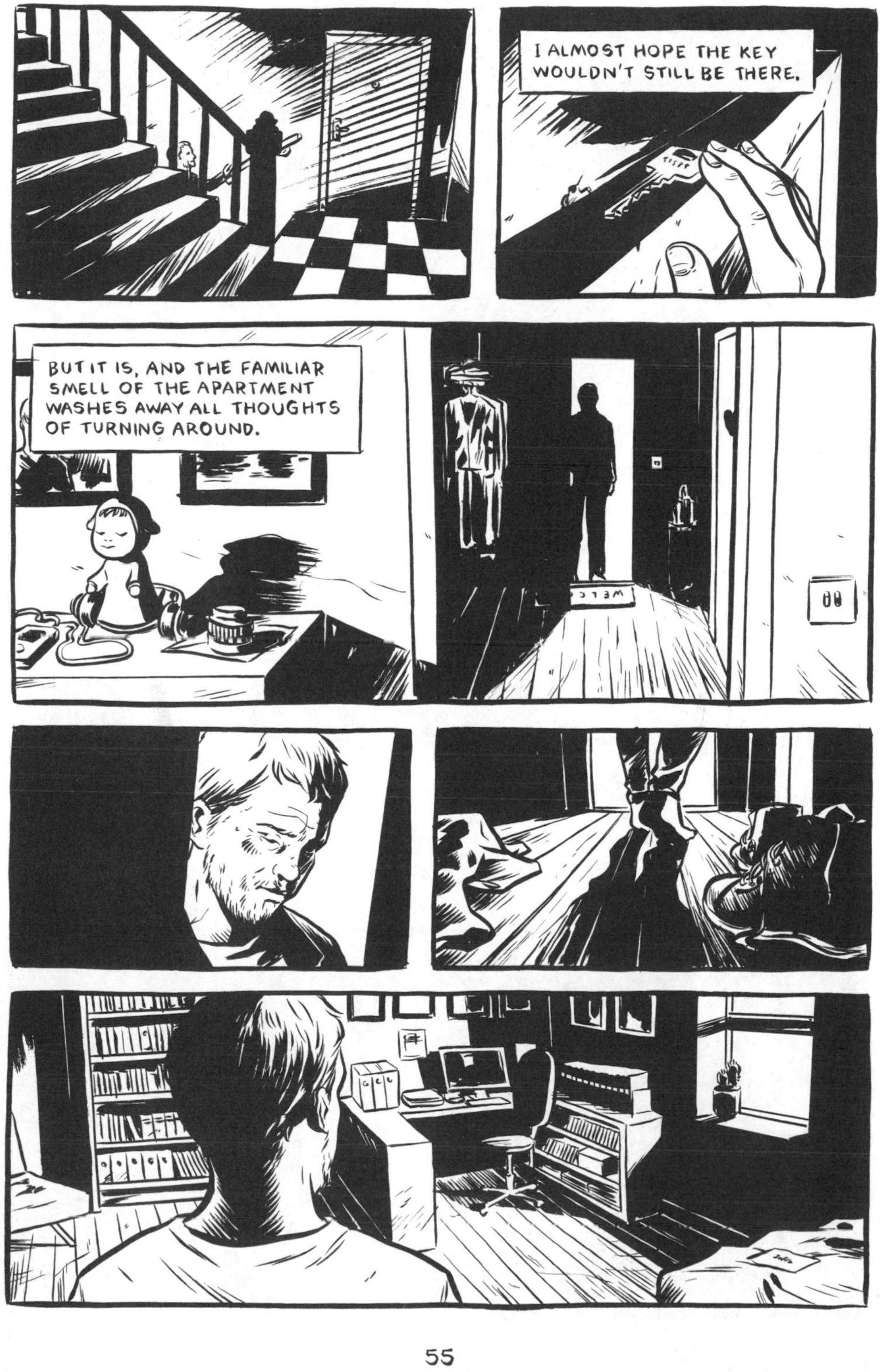
I ALMOST HOPE THE KEY WOULDN'T STILL BE THERE.
BUT IT IS, AND THE FAMILIAR SMELL OF THE APARTMENT WASHES AWAY ALL THOUGHTS OF TURNING AROUND.

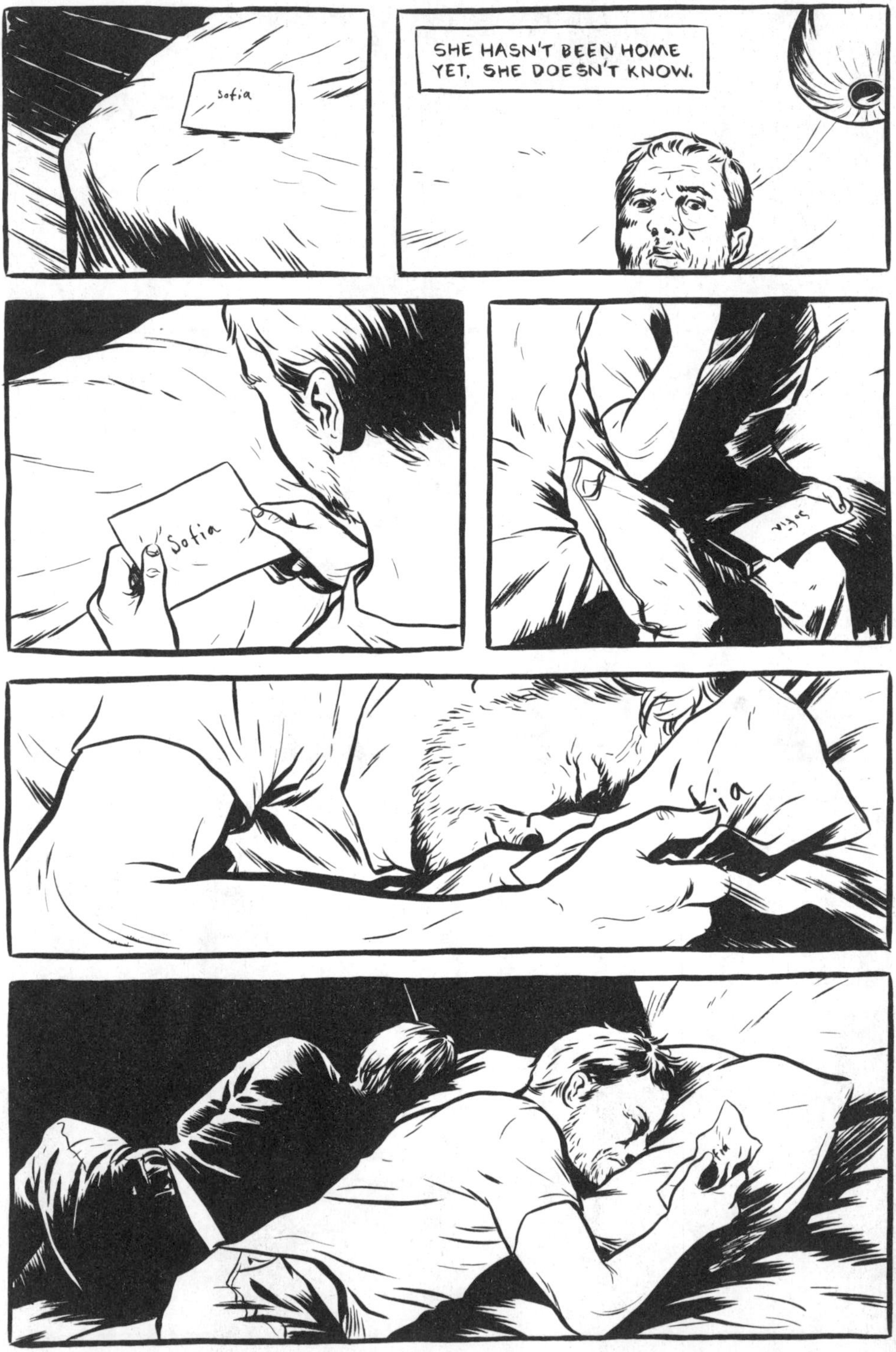
sofia
SHE HASN'T BEEN HOME YET. SHE DOESN'T KNOW.
Sofia

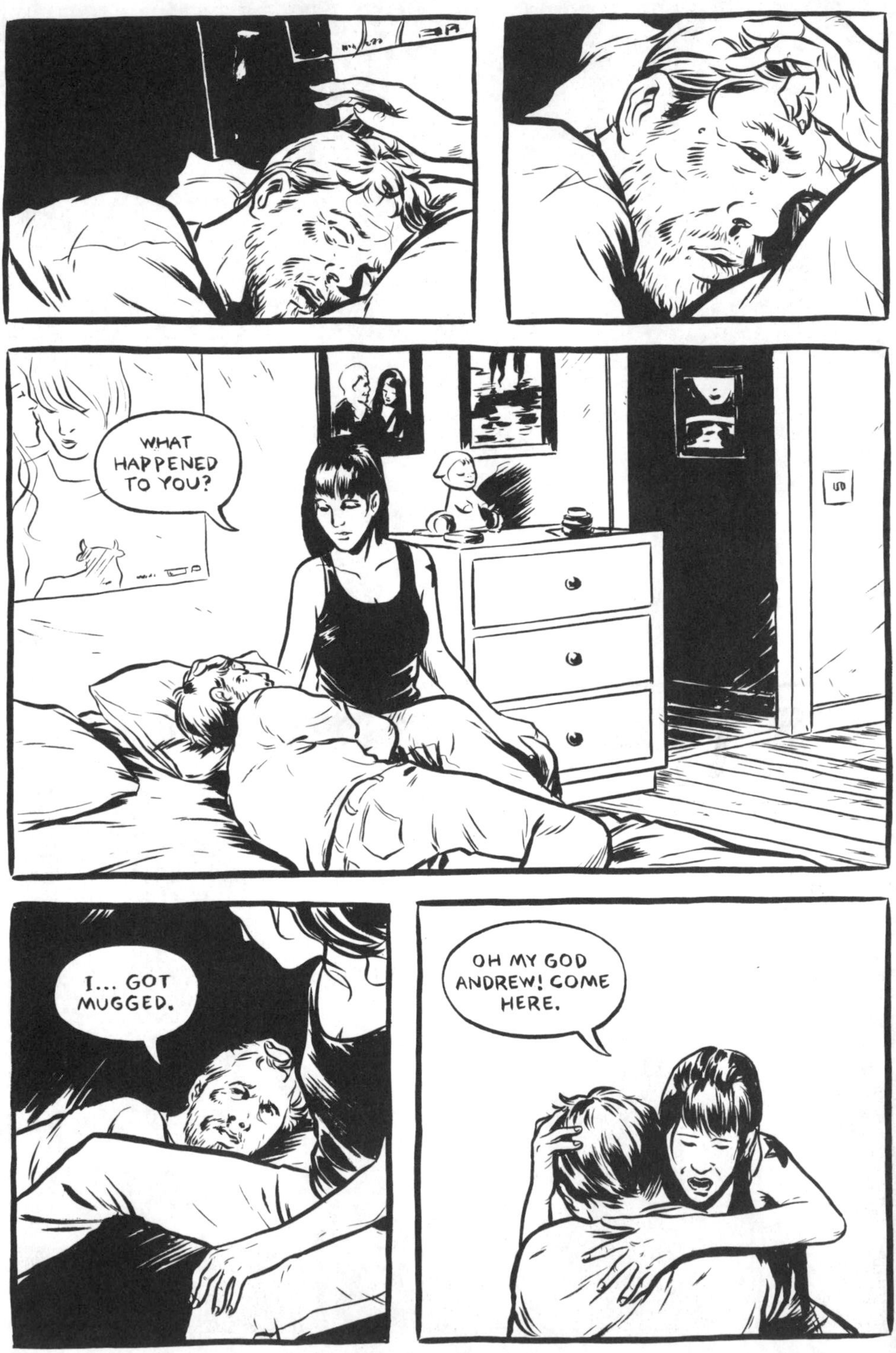
WHAT HAPPENED TO YOU?
I... GOT MUGGED.
OH MY GOD ANDREW! COME HERE.

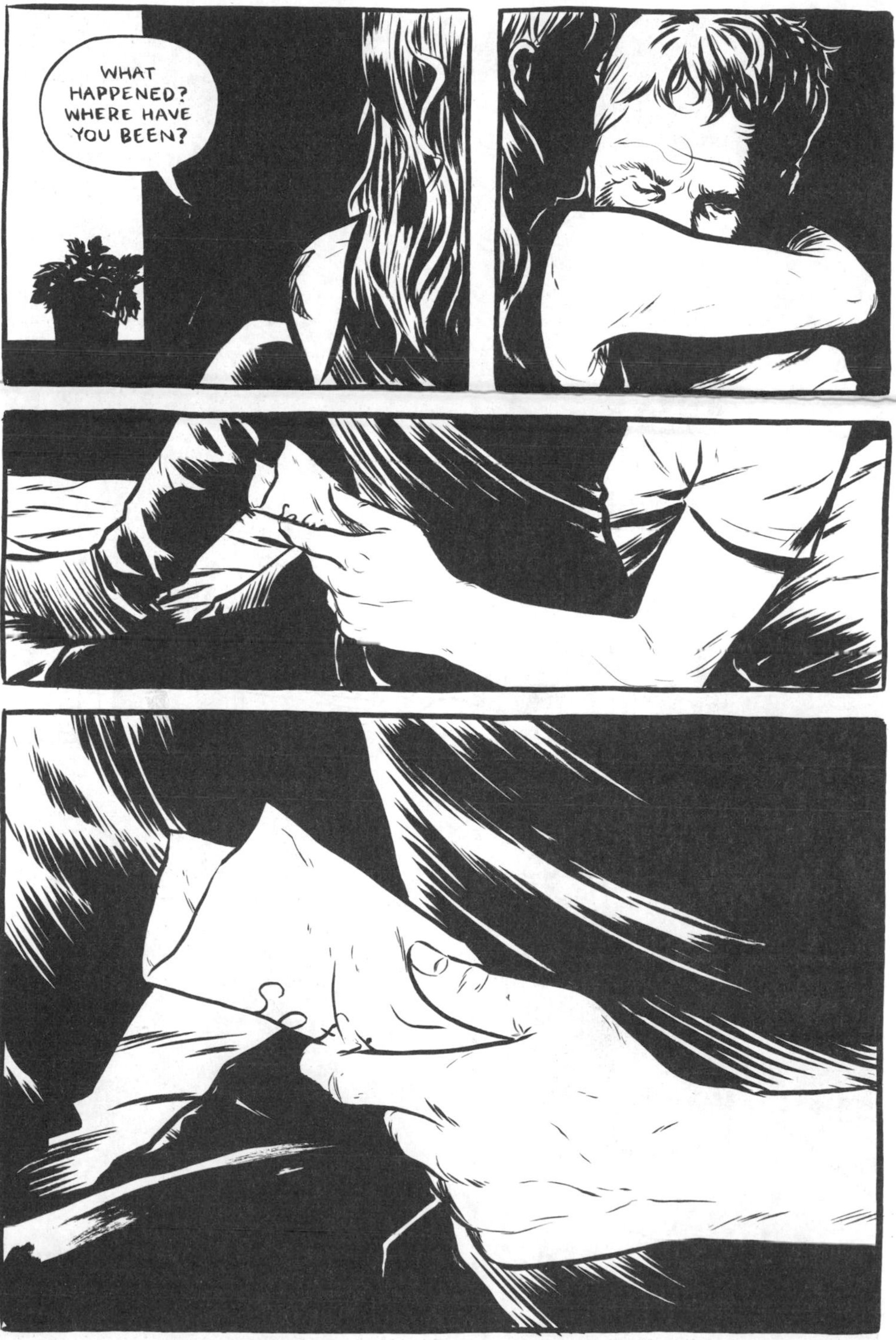
WHAT HAPPENED? WHERE HAVE YOU BEEN?

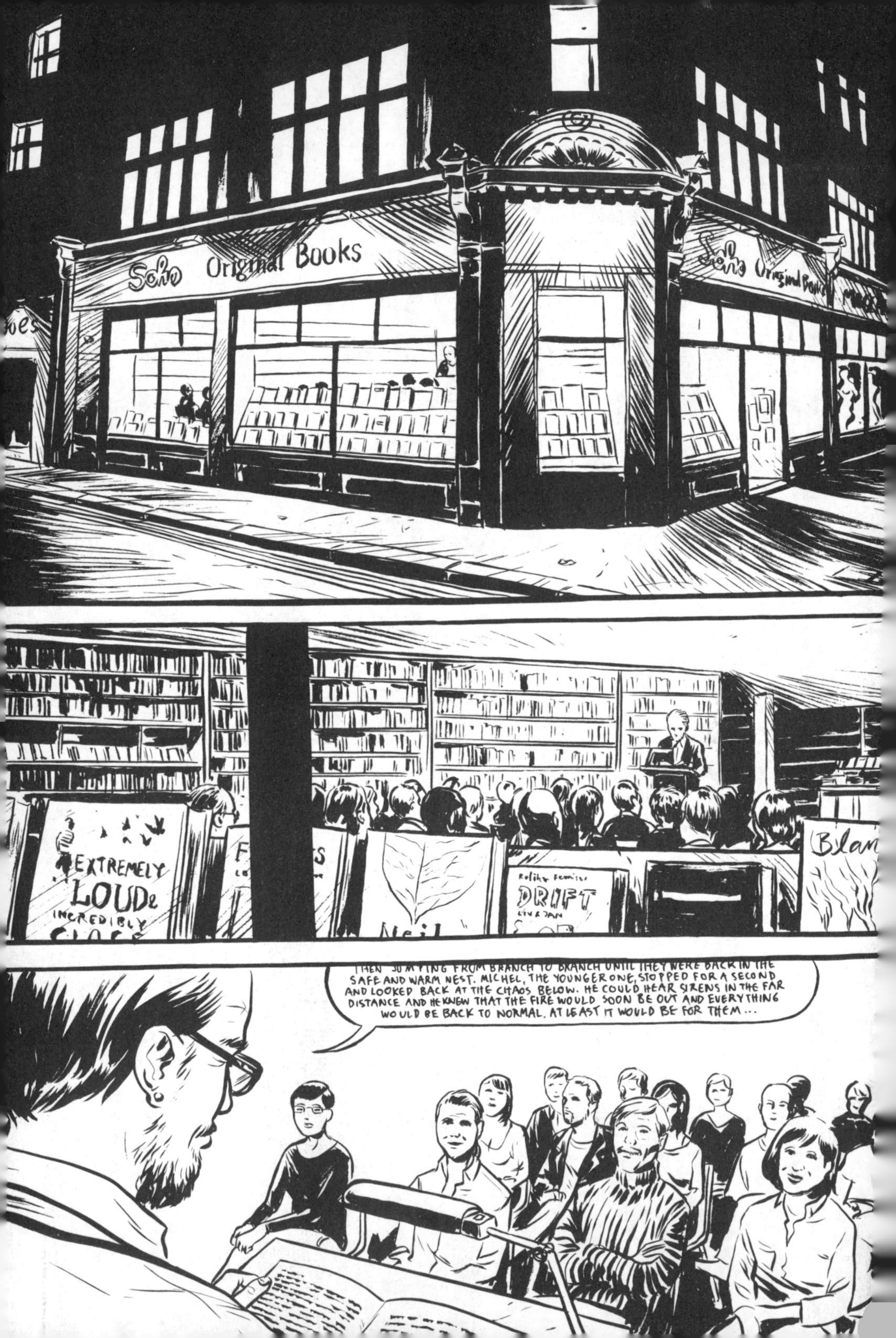

Soho Original Books
Soho Original Books
EXTREMELY LOUD INCREDIBLY
DRIFT
Neil
Blan
THEN JUMPING FROM BRANCH TO BRANCH UNTIL THEY WERE BACK IN THE SAFE AND WARM NEST. MICHEL, THE YOUNGER ONE, STOPPED FOR A SECOND AND LOOKED BACK AT THE CHAOS BELOW. HE COULD HEAR SIRENS IN THE FAR DISTANCE AND HE KNEW THAT THE FIRE WOULD SOON BE OUT AND EVERYTHING WOULD BE BACK TO NORMAL. AT LEAST IT WOULD BE FOR THEM...

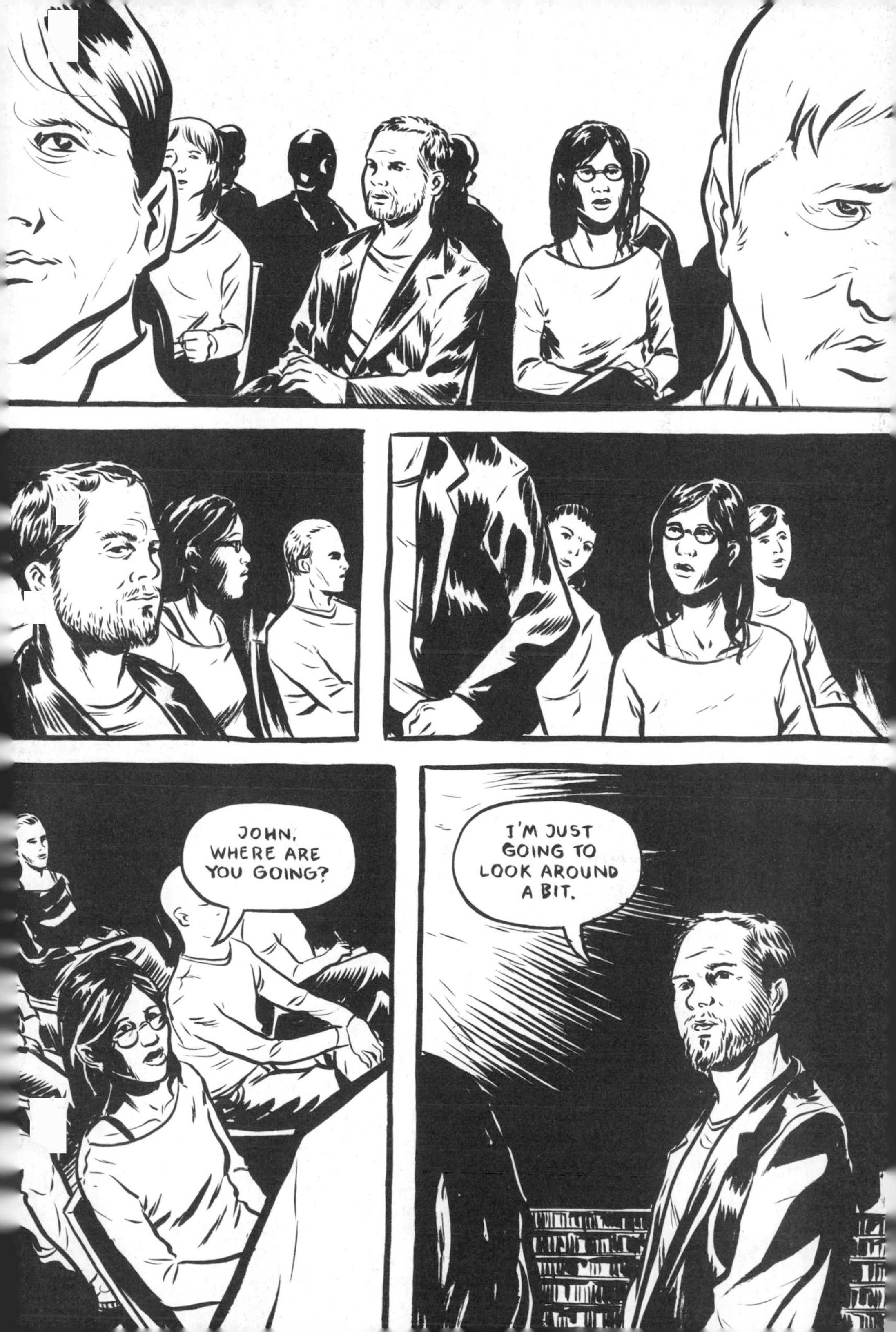
JOHN, WHERE ARE YOU GOING?
I'M JUST GOING TO LOOK AROUND A BIT.

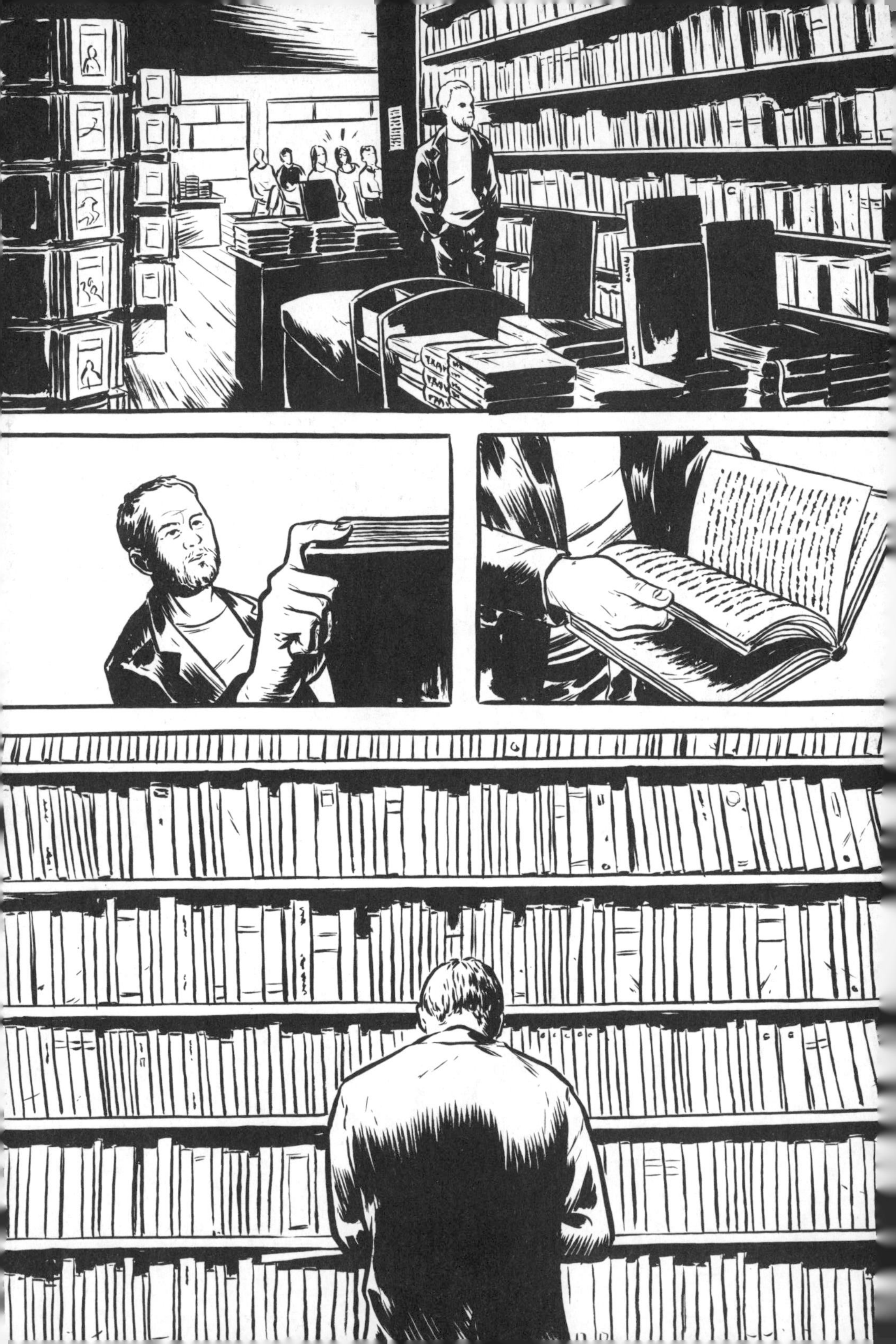

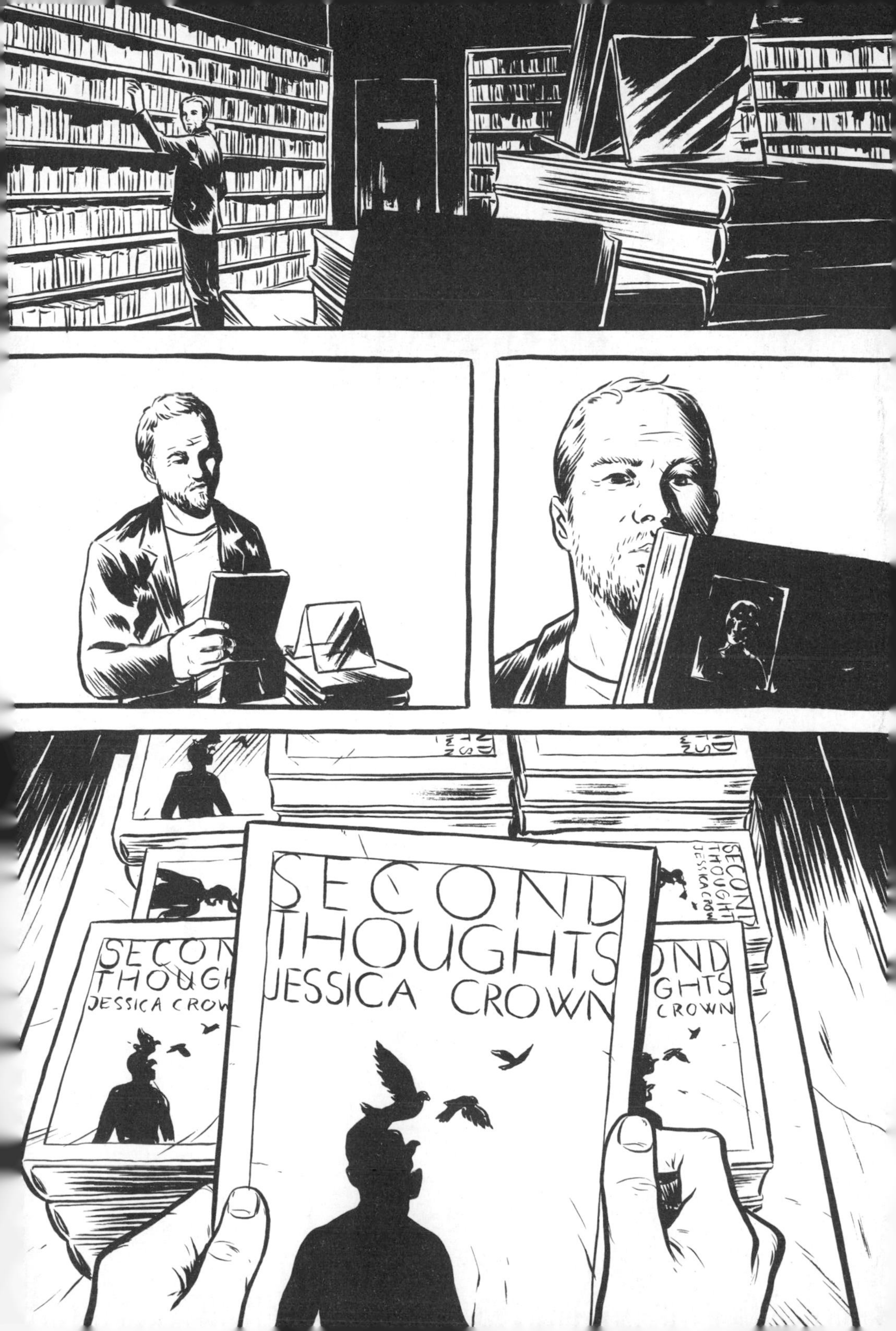
SECOND THOUGHTS
JESSICA CROWN

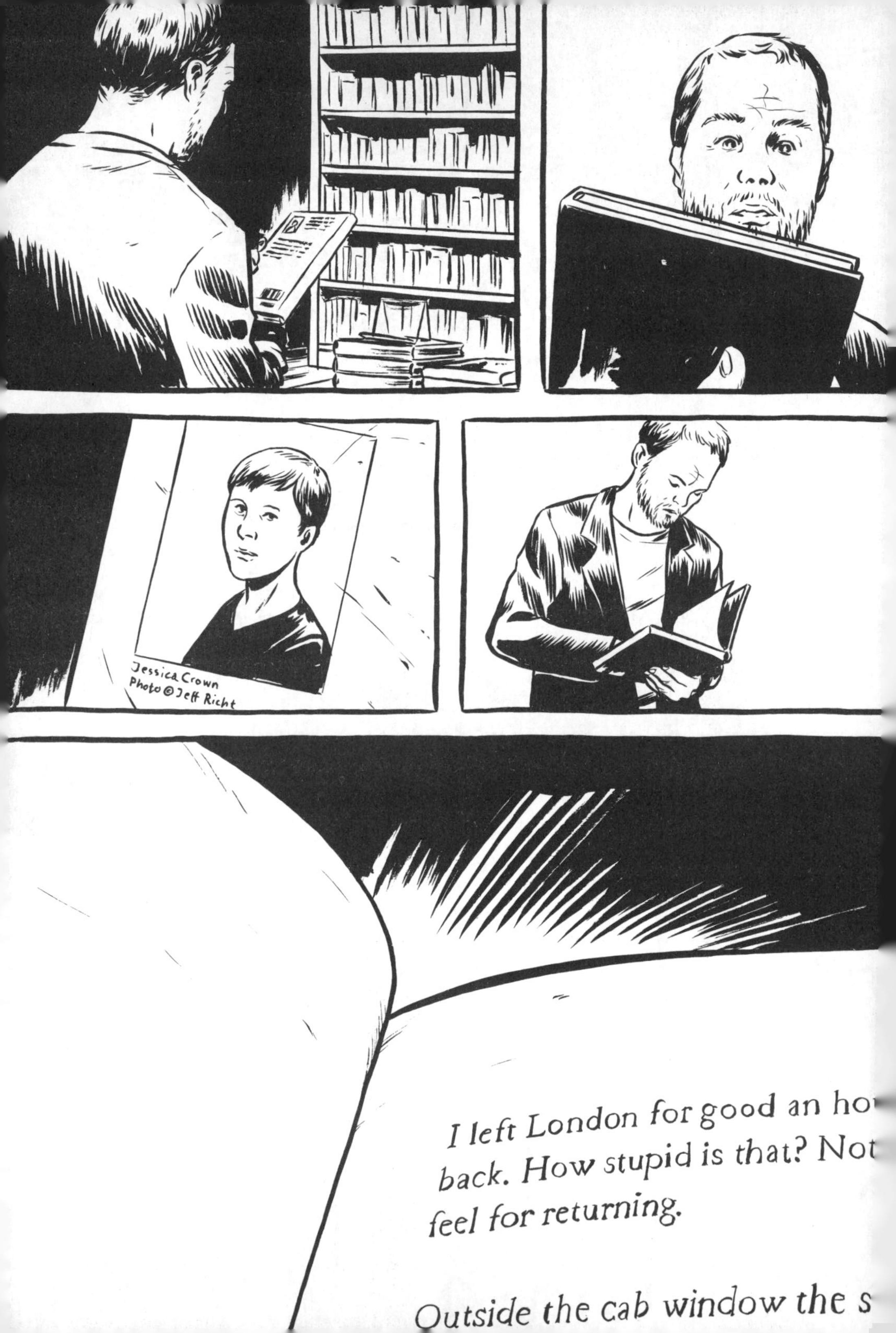
Jessica Crown
Photo © Jeff Richt
I left London for good an ho
back. How stupid is that? Not
feel for returning.
Outside the cab window the s

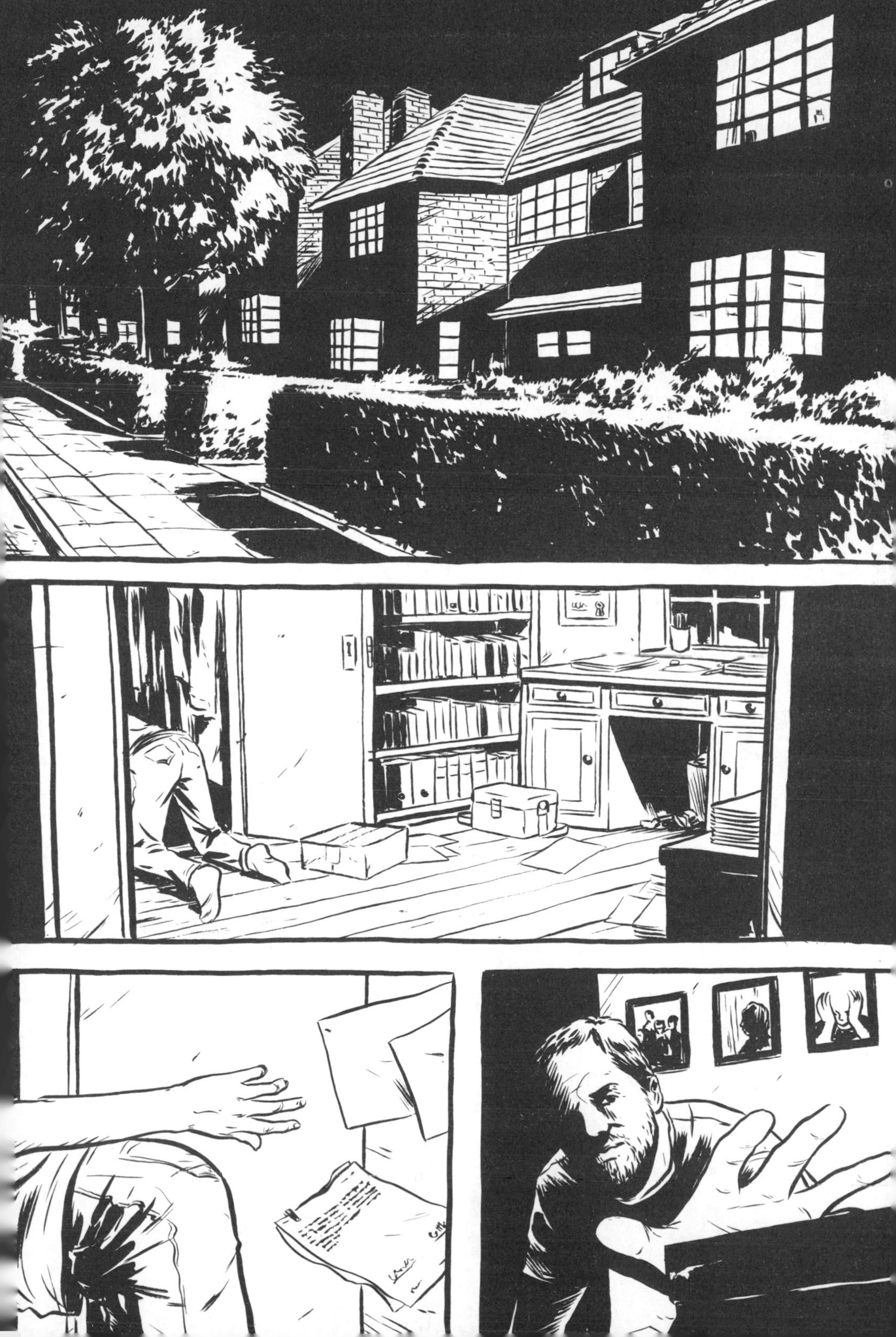

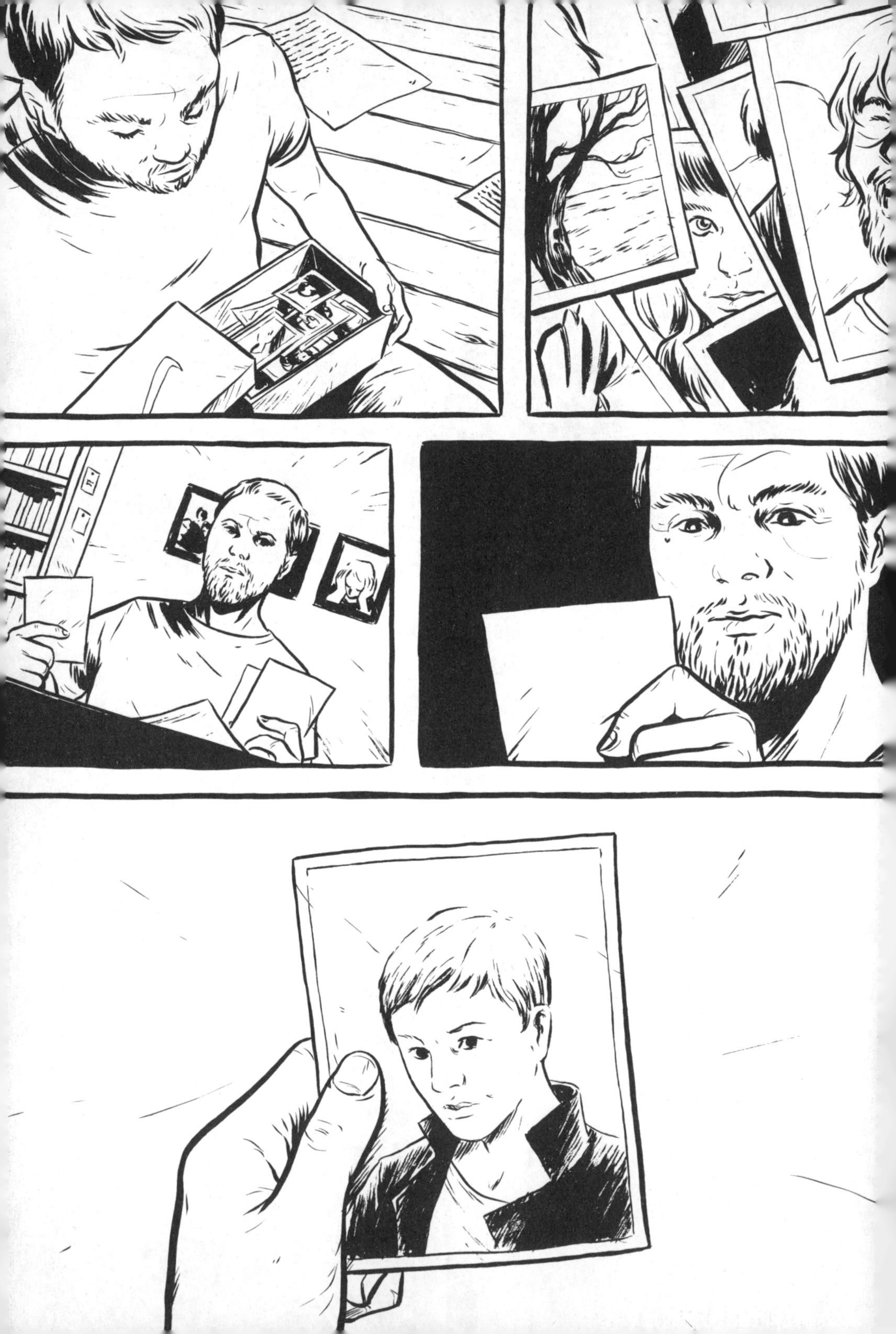

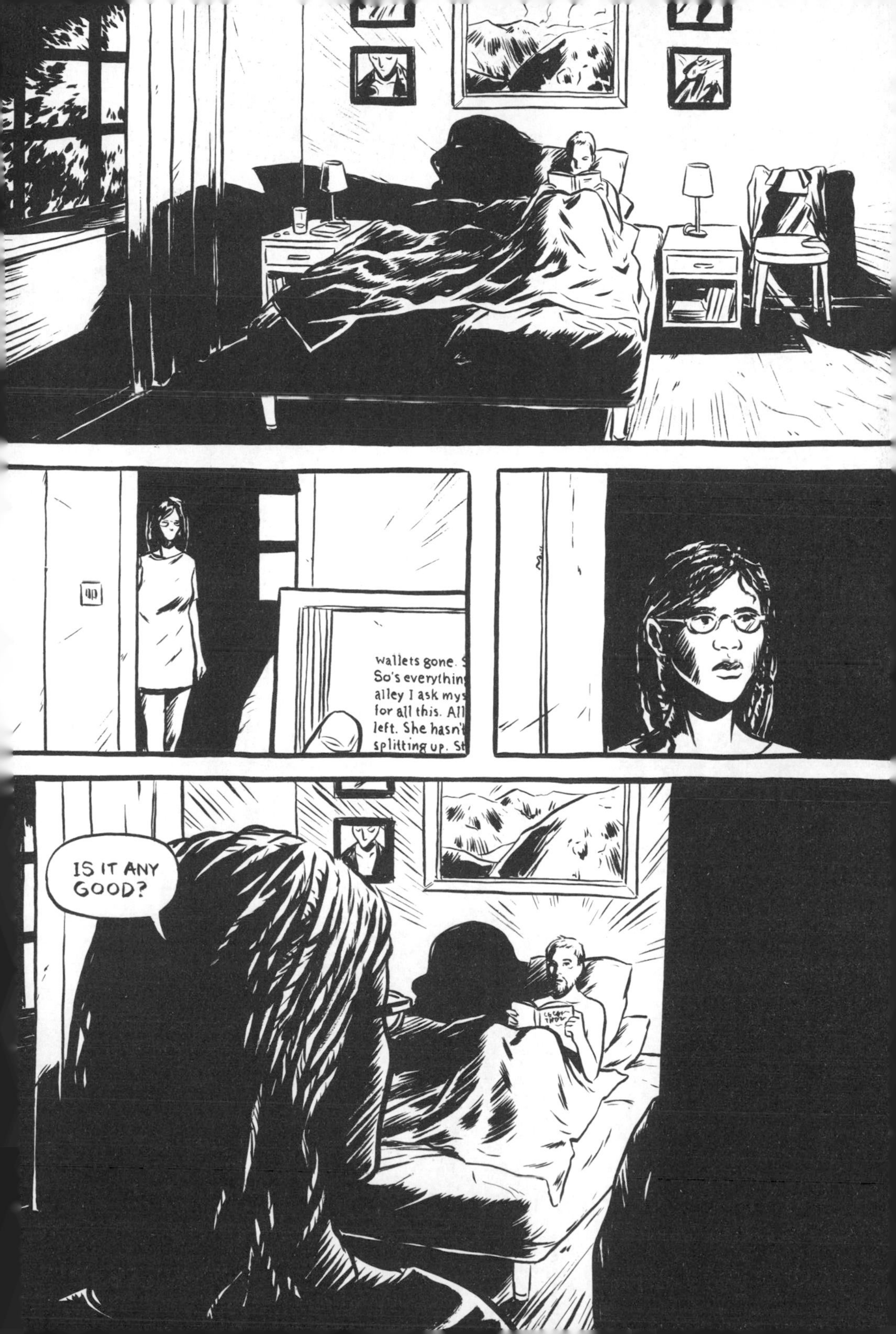
wallets gone. S
So's everythin
alley I ask mys
for all this. All
left. She hasn't
splitting up. St
IS IT ANY GOOD?

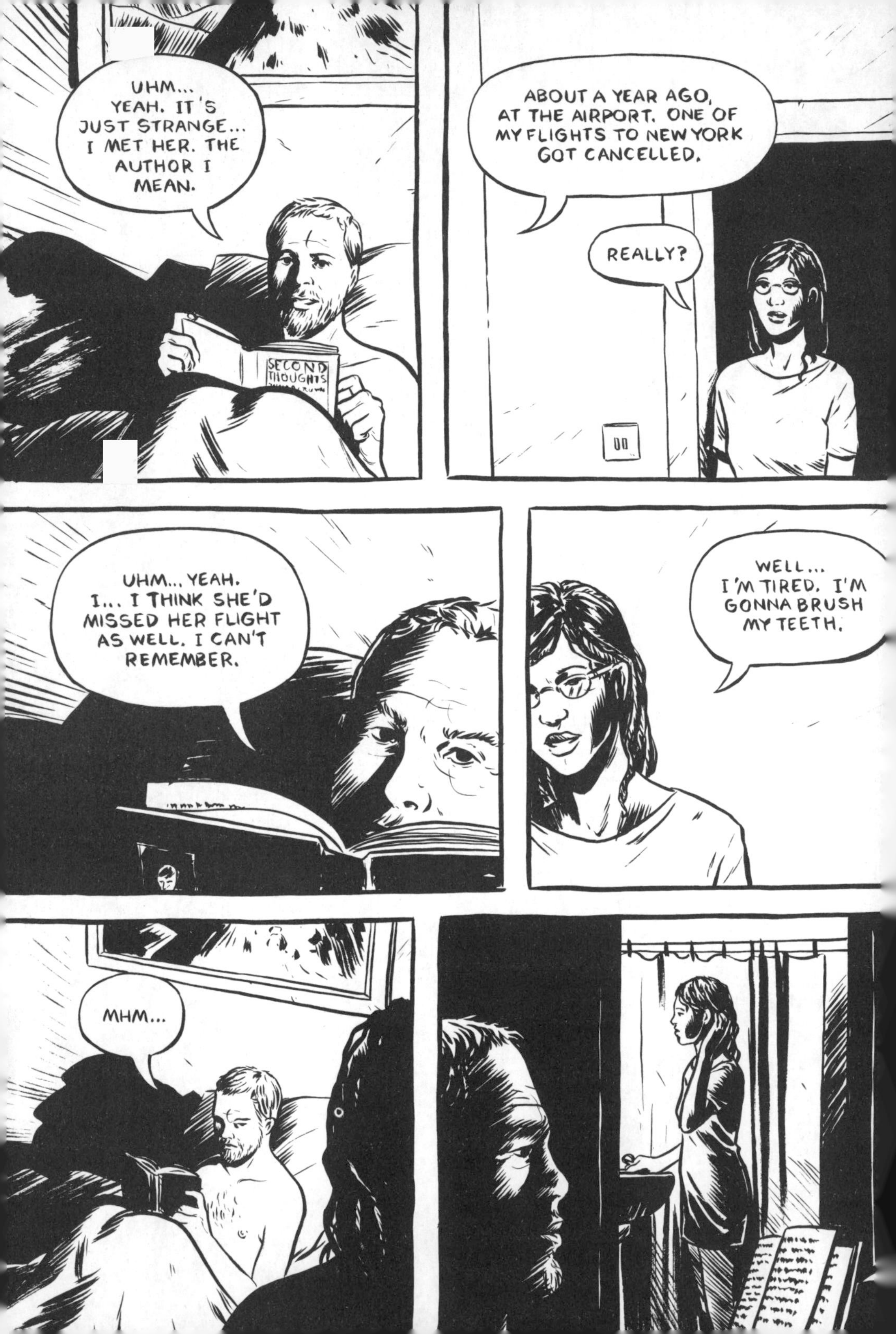
UHM... YEAH. IT'S JUST STRANGE... I MET HER. THE AUTHOR I MEAN.
SECOND THOUGHTS
ABOUT A YEAR AGO, AT THE AIRPORT. ONE OF MY FLIGHTS TO NEW YORK GOT CANCELLED.
REALLY?
UHM... YEAH. I... I THINK SHE'D MISSED HER FLIGHT AS WELL. I CAN'T REMEMBER.
WELL... I'M TIRED. I'M GONNA BRUSH MY TEETH.
MHM...

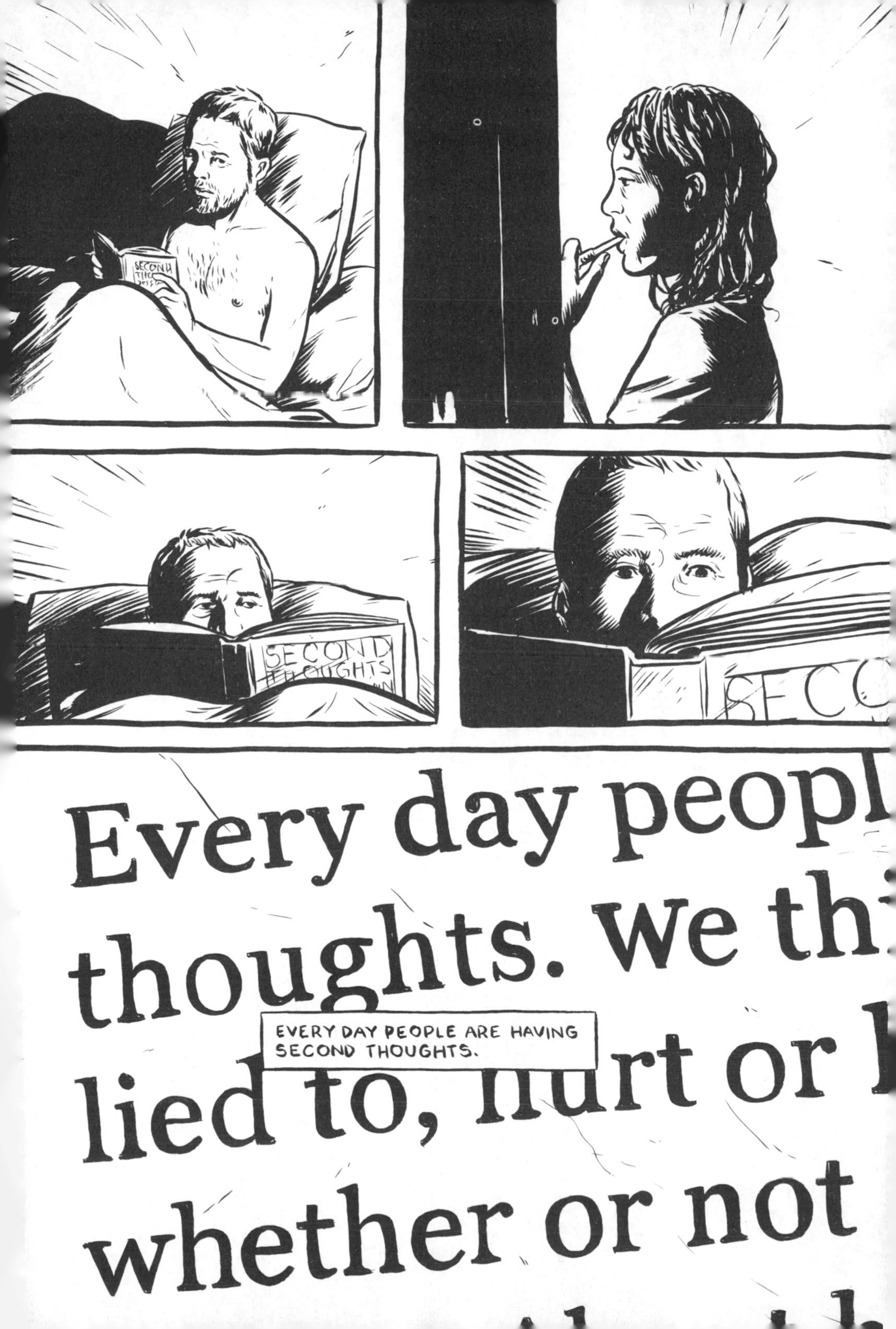
SECOND THOUGHTS
Every day peopl
thoughts. We thi
lied to, hurt or
whether or not
EVERY DAY PEOPLE ARE HAVING SECOND THOUGHTS.

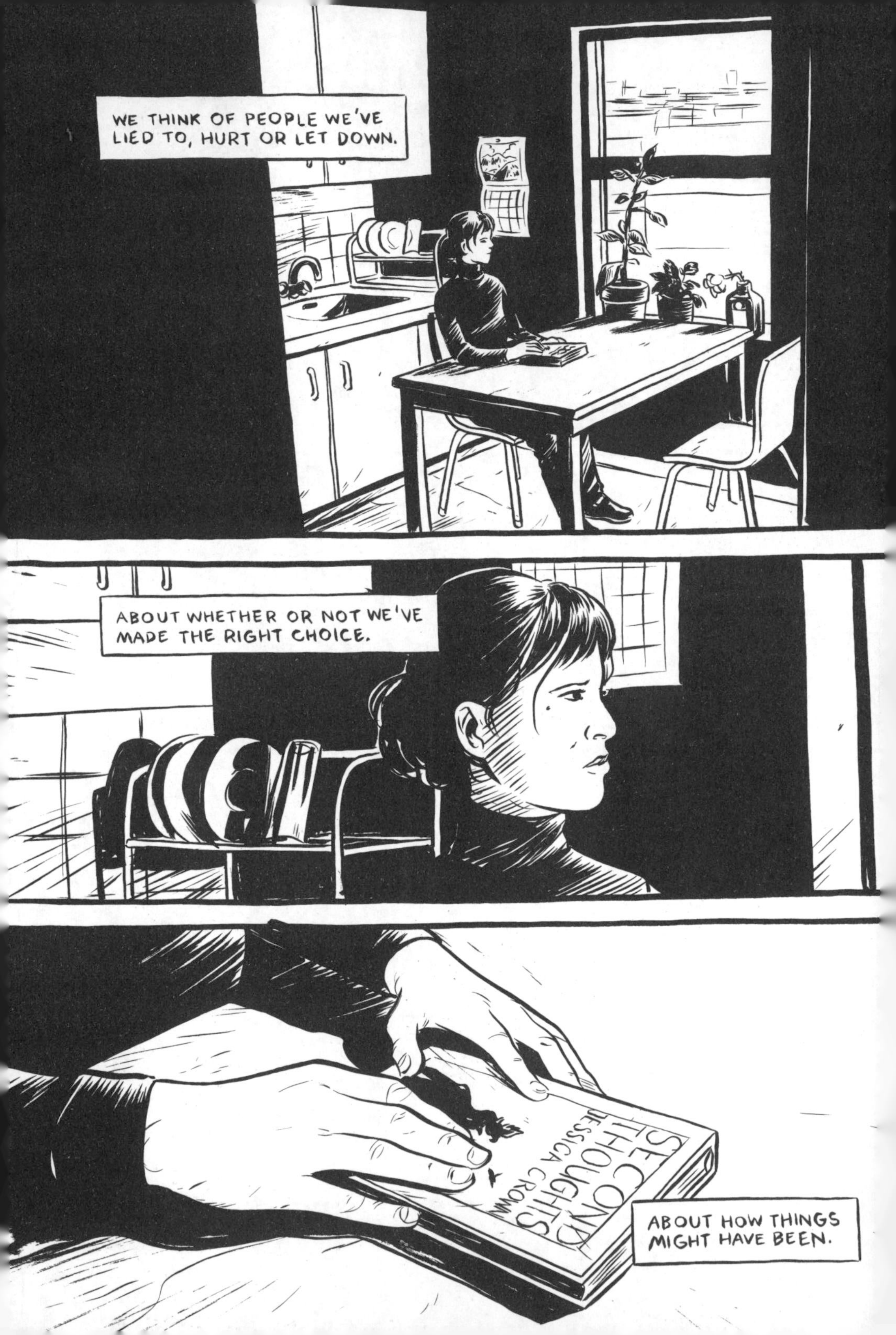
WE THINK OF PEOPLE WE'VE LIED TO, HURT OR LET DOWN.
ABOUT WHETHER OR NOT WE'VE MADE THE RIGHT CHOICE.
SECOND THOUGHTS
JESSICA CROWN
ABOUT HOW THINGS MIGHT HAVE BEEN.

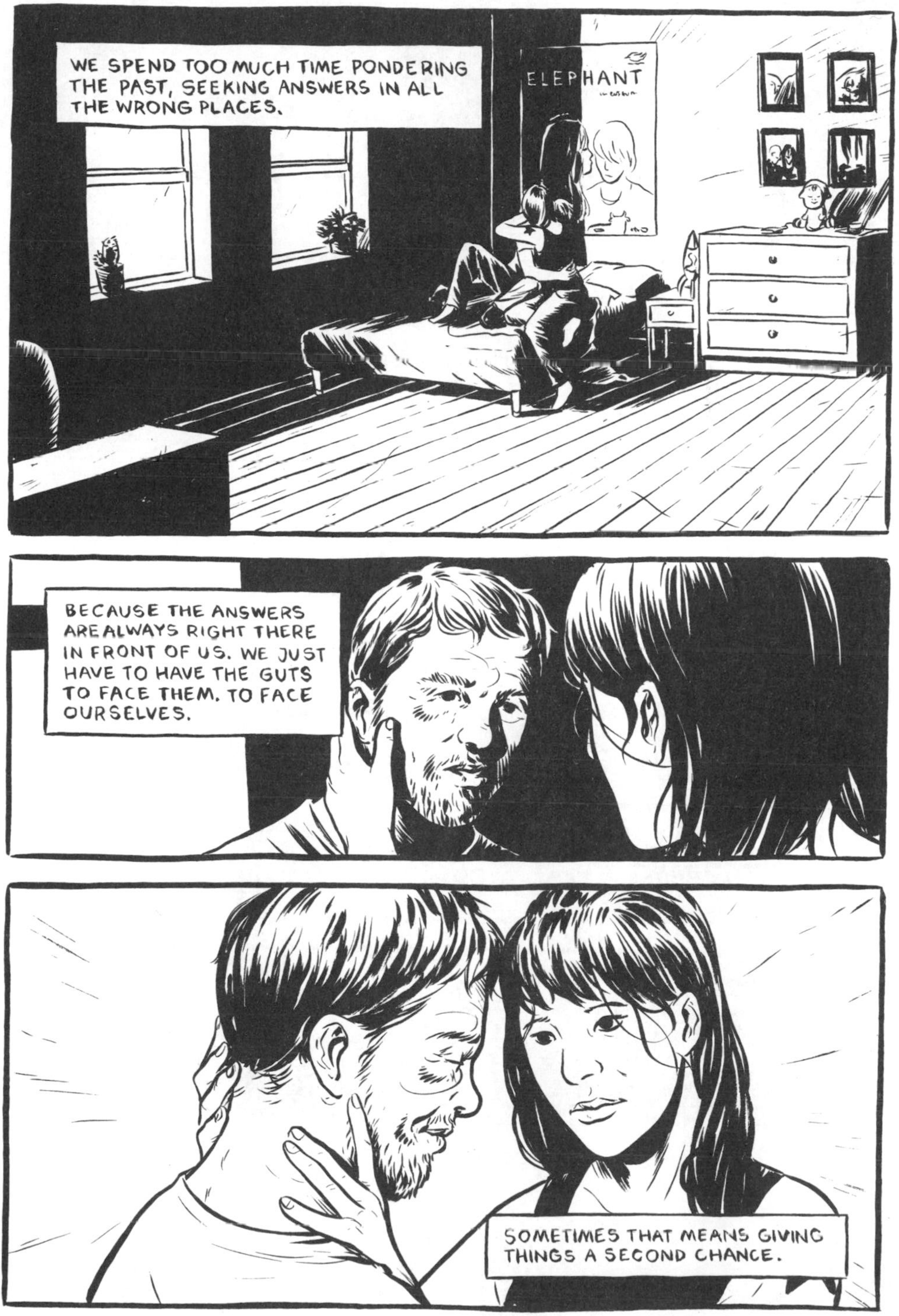
WE SPEND TOO MUCH TIME PONDERING THE PAST, SEEKING ANSWERS IN ALL THE WRONG PLACES.
ELEPHANT
BECAUSE THE ANSWERS ARE ALWAYS RIGHT THERE IN FRONT OF US. WE JUST HAVE TO HAVE THE GUTS TO FACE THEM. TO FACE OURSELVES.
SOMETIMES THAT MEANS GIVING THINGS A SECOND CHANCE.

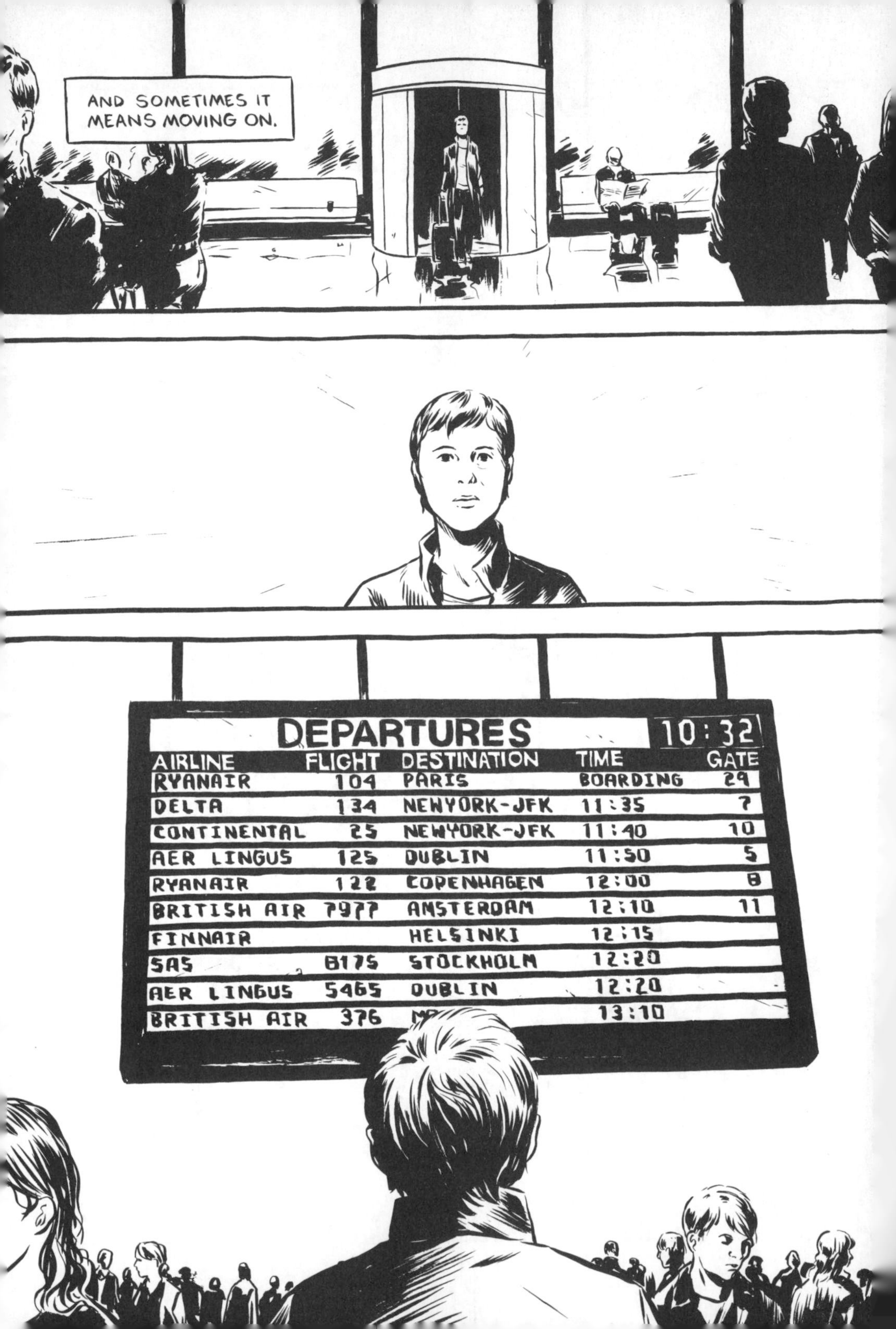
AND SOMETIMES IT MEANS MOVING ON.
DEPARTURES 10:32
AIRLINE FLIGHT DESTINATION TIME GATE
RYANAIR 104 PARIS BOARDING 29
DELTA 134 NEWYORK-JFK 11:35 7
CONTINENTAL 25 NEWYORK-JFK 11:40 10
AER LINGUS 125 DUBLIN 11:50 5
RYANAIR 122 COPENHAGEN 12:00 8
BRITISH AIR 7977 AMSTERDAM 12:10 11
FINNAIR HELSINKI 12:15
SAS 6175 STOCKHOLM 12:20
AER LINGUS 5465 DUBLIN 12:20
BRITISH AIR 376 13:10

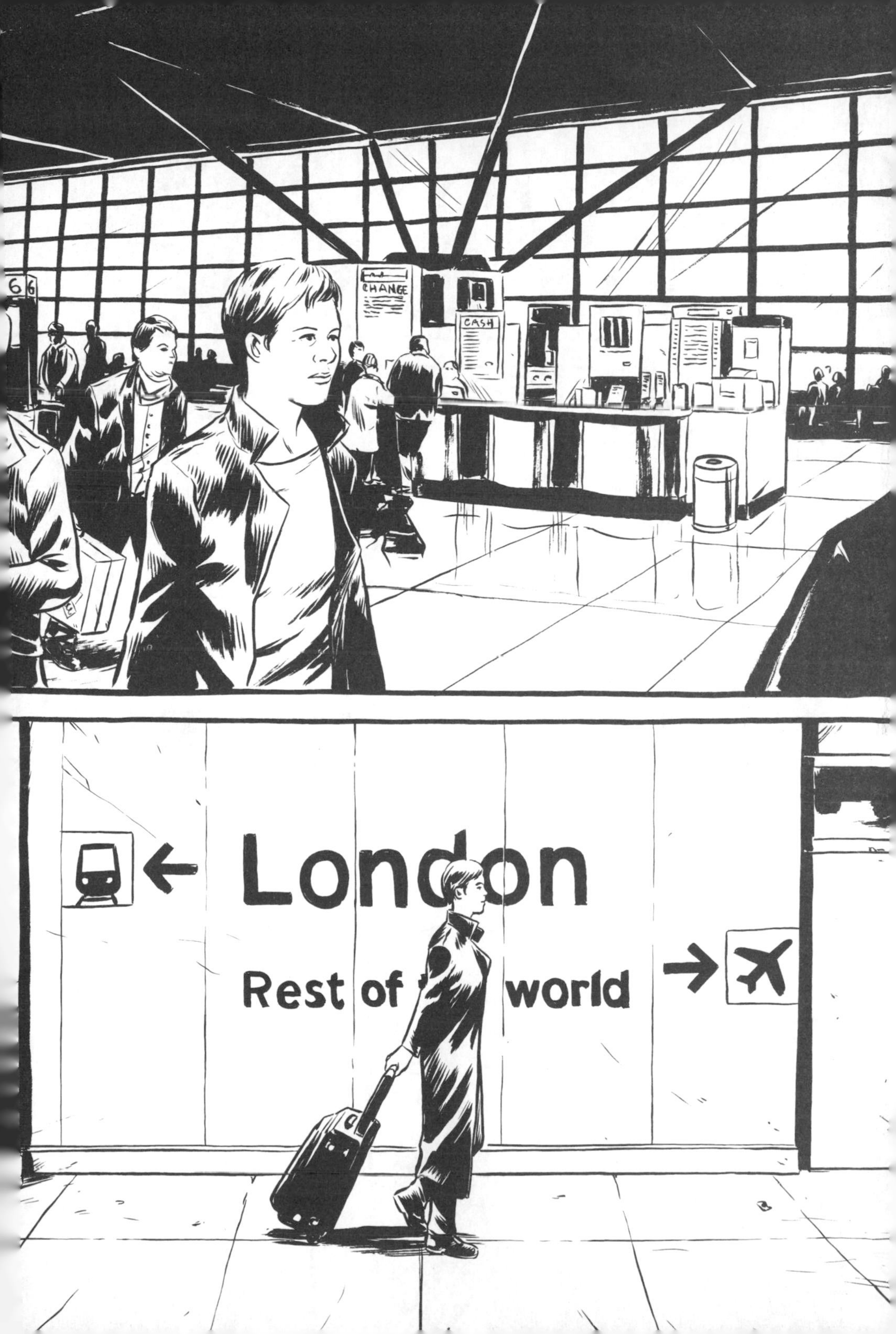
6
6
CHANGE
CASH
London
Rest of
world

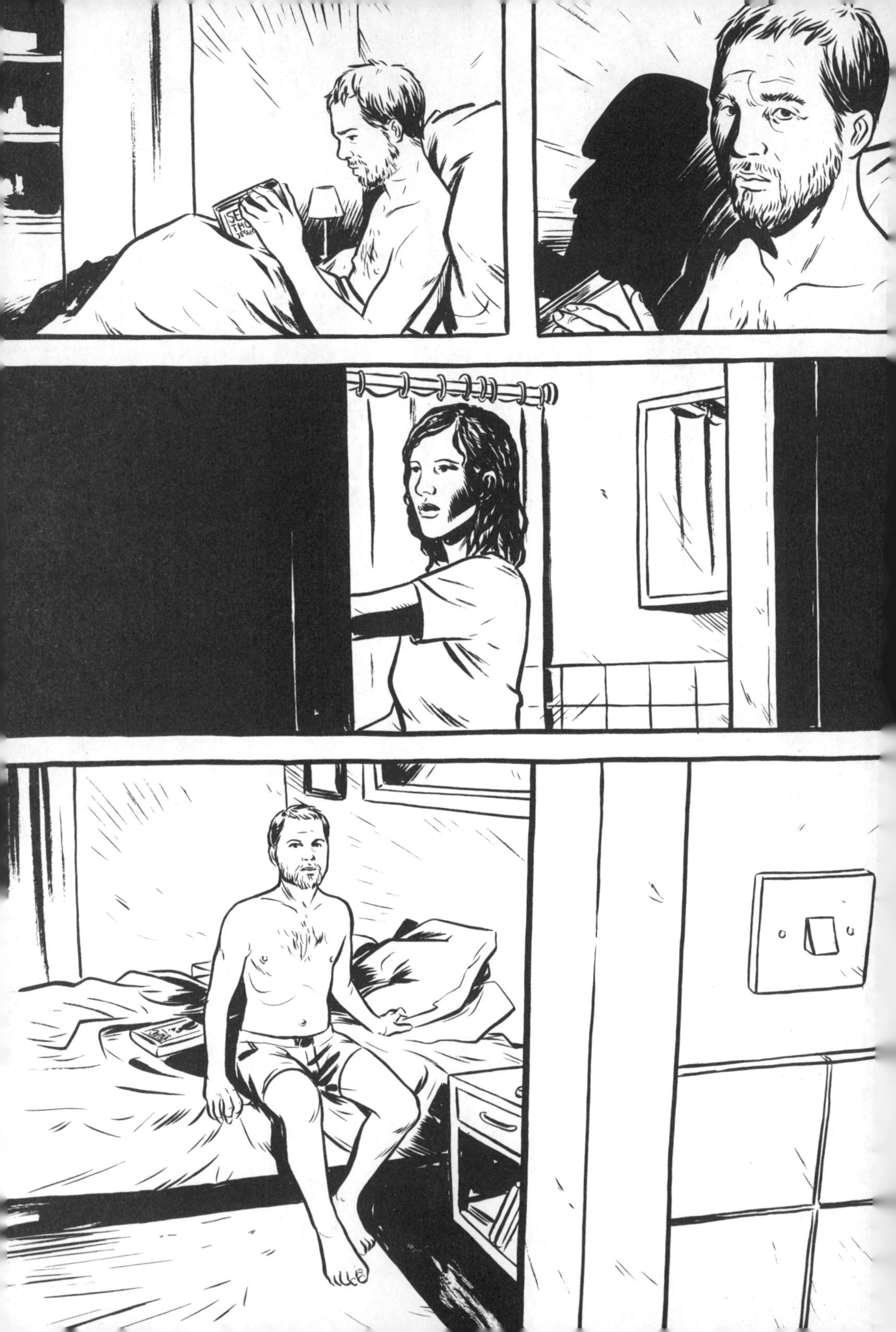

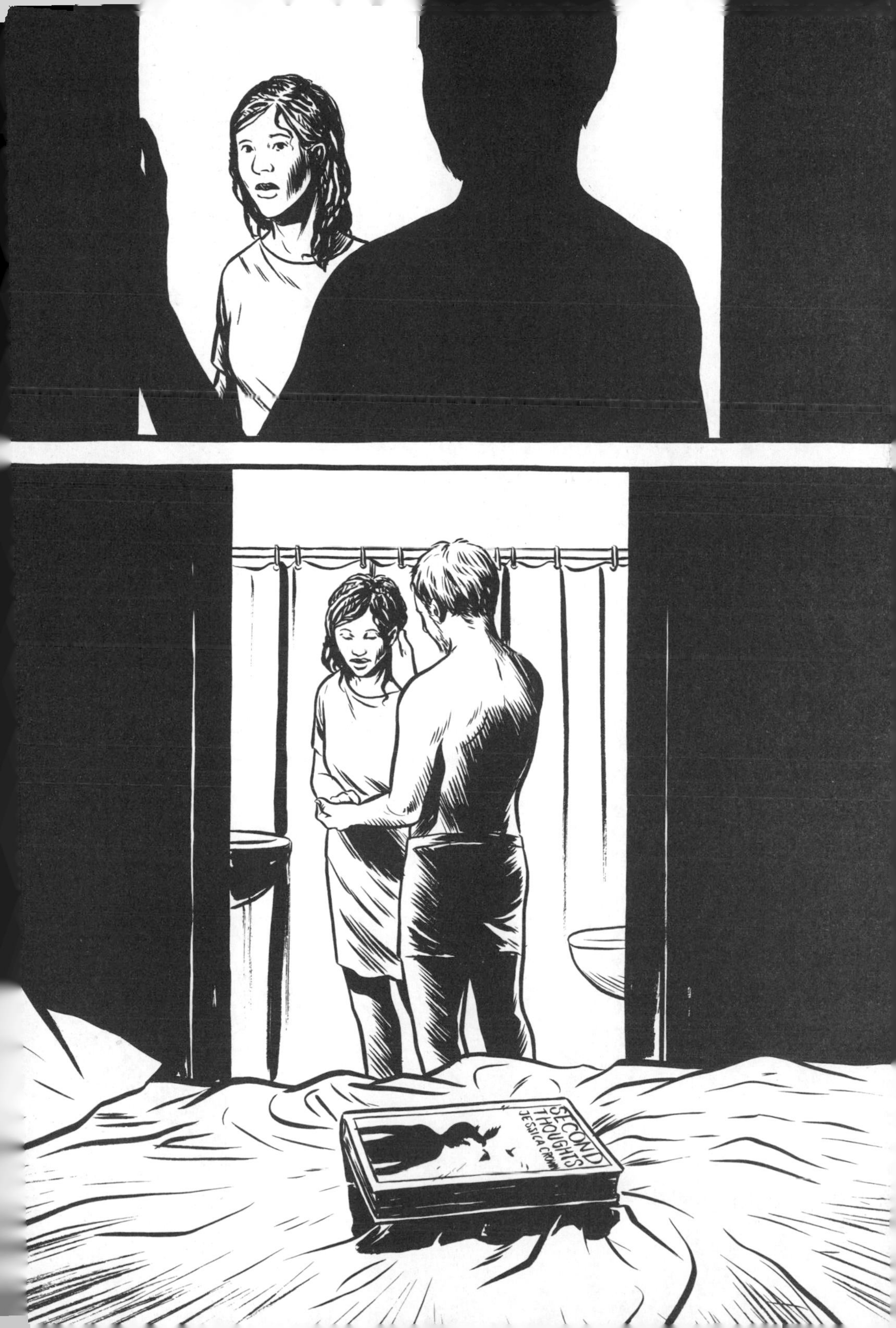
SECOND THOUGHTS
JESSICA

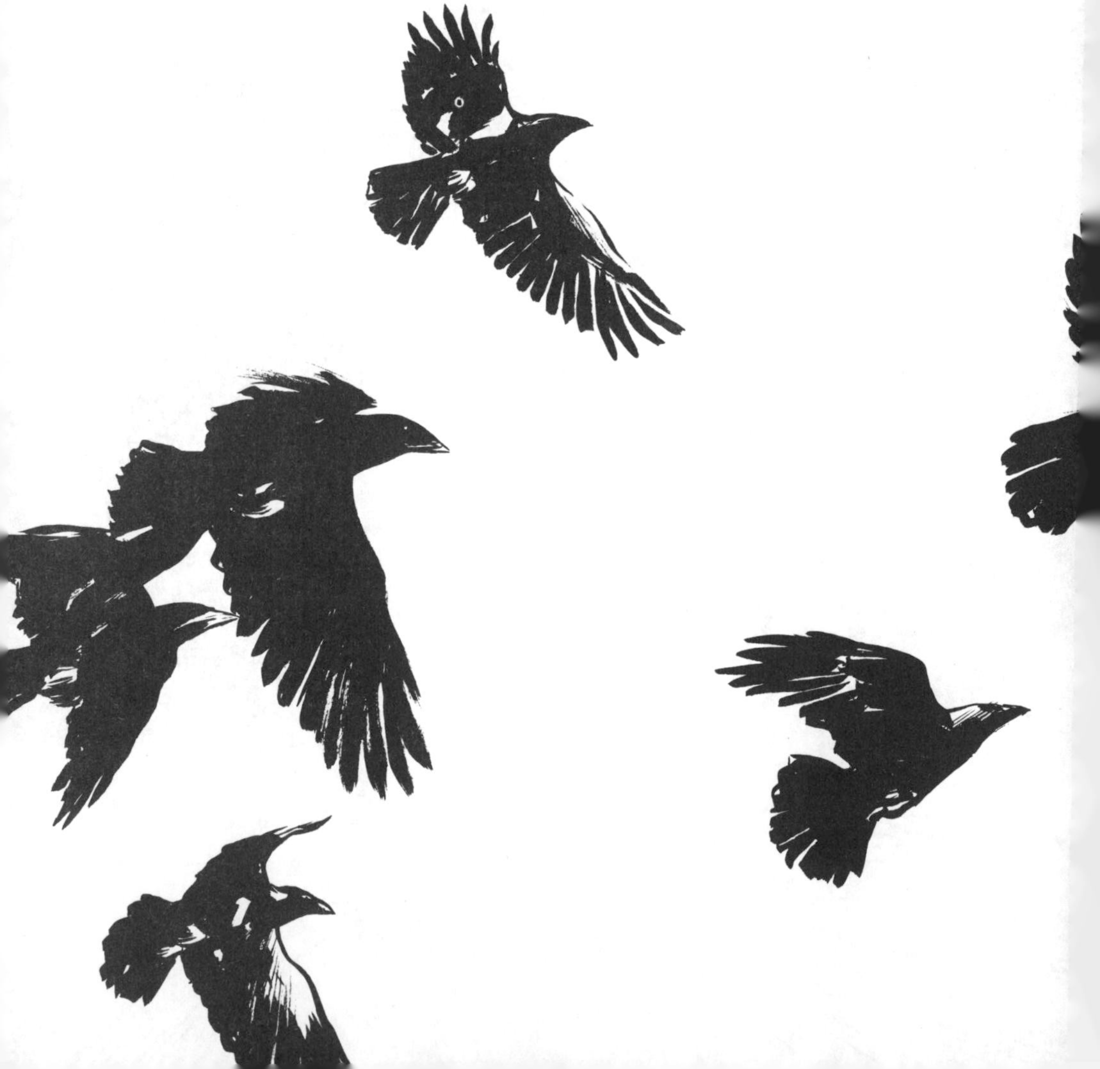

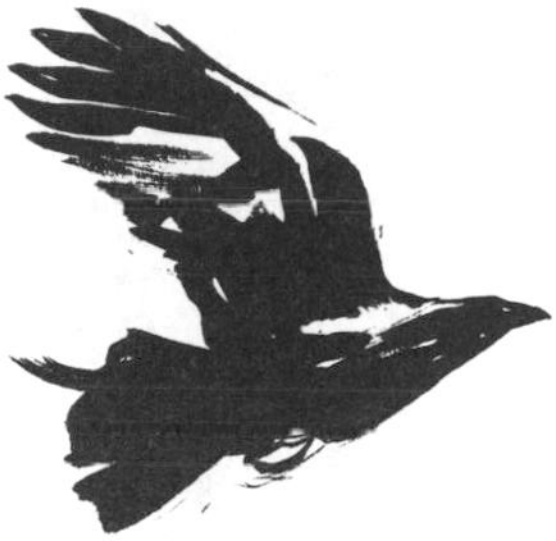
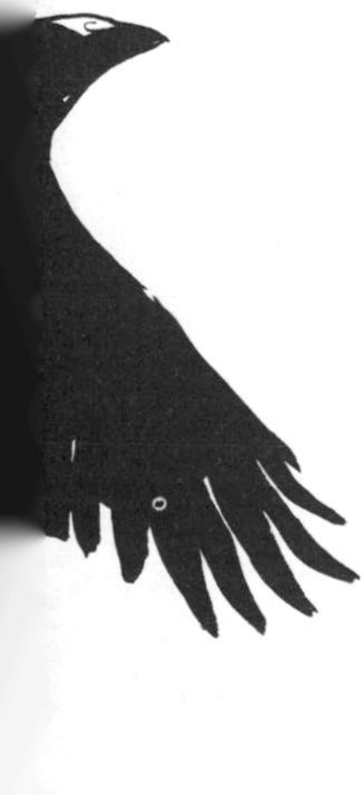

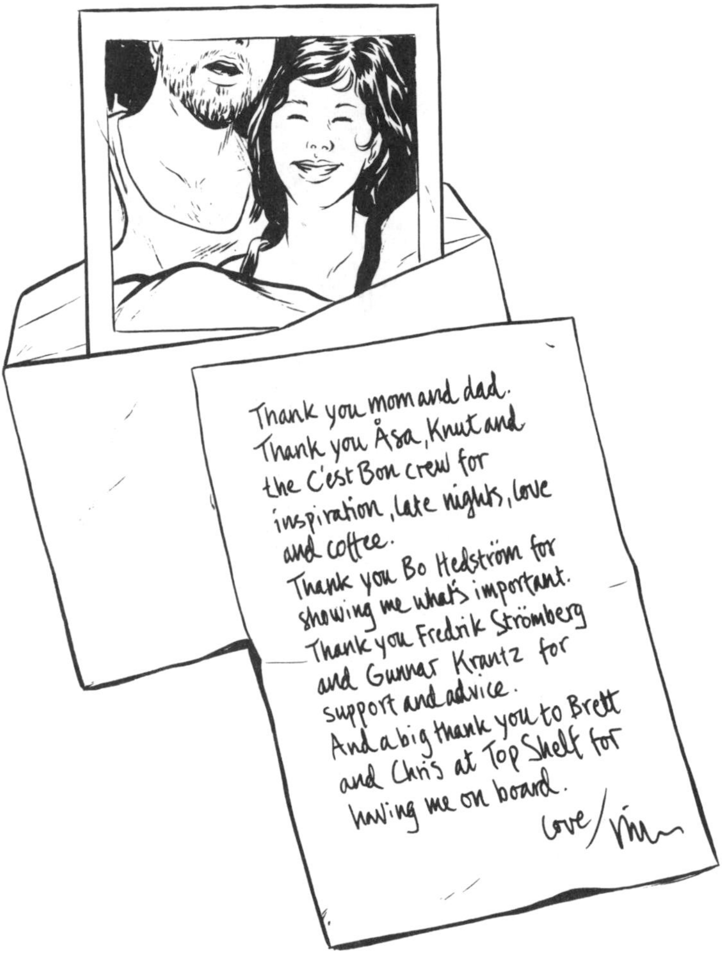
Thank you mom and dad.
Thank you Åsa, Knut and
the C'est Bon crew for
inspiration, late nights, love
and coffee.
Thank you Bo Hedström for
showing me what's important.
Thank you Fredrik Strömberg
and Gunnar Krantz for
support and advice.
And a big thank you to Brett
and Chris at Top Shelf for
having me on board.
Love/